Bourbon Leader:
Grover Cleveland
and the
Democratic Party

The Library of American Biography

EDITED BY OSCAR HANDLIN

Horace Samuel Merrill

Bourbon Leader:
Grover Cleveland
and the
Democratic Party

Edited by Oscar Handlin

Little, Brown and Company · *Boston* · *Toronto*

*Published simultaneously in Canada
by Little, Brown & Company (Canada) Limited*

PRINTED IN THE UNITED STATES OF AMERICA

To
"Mom" and "Pop" Galbraith

Acknowledgments

SEVERAL people aided me in the preparation of this book. Two in particular deserve special recognition. One is my wife, who helped with research, typed and retyped, edited and re-edited as though obsessed. I am also deeply indebted to Oscar Handlin, whose superior ability as an editor has been both an inspiration and a very real help.

Other individuals aided me in certain aspects of the project. Among these were Frank Freidel, Professor of History at Harvard University, and Wesley M. Gewehr, Chairman of the History Department at the University of Maryland. Two of my graduate students contributed significant information: Guy Goodfellow, who educated me on Cleveland's legal career, and Marshall Brement, who helped me to a better understanding of Samuel J. Tilden. I sincerely thank all of you.

HORACE SAMUEL MERRILL

Editor's Preface

FOR SOME twenty years after the Civil War, one party effectively controlled the federal government of the United States. The Democratic party through those decades was excluded from power by the collapse of its organization after 1860, by the effects of Reconstruction, and by the persistent stigma of disloyalty.

Many Americans believed that a revival of the Democracy was essential to an effective two-party system. Yet the party seemed condemned to minority status. It survived only because it still clung to certain bastions of strength in the state and local governments.

Within it there clustered a variety of discontented groups. By the very fact that it was always in opposition, it drew to it men of every sort with grievances against the dominant Republican party. The aggrieved groups were themselves disparate; they could join in opposition, but it was not clear they had enough in common to unite in a positive program should they regain control of the government.

In 1884 the party included in its ranks many farmers,

severely hit by a long agricultural depression and eager for radical measures of relief. By their side were some urban laborers, particularly those of immigrant descent entrenched in the city machines. Some respectable men of wealth and status found themselves in the opposition by reason of family loyalties or hostility to the protectionist policy of the G.O.P. Finally, miscellaneous groups of reformers, interested in good government, were antagonized by the corruption and ineffectiveness of the party in power. These groups, pursuing goals that were often contradictory and ever suspicious of one another, were as ready to fall into factional disputes as to battle the common enemy.

The critical test came when the party did return to power in 1884. It was significant that it did so under the leadership of Grover Cleveland, whose distinctive career had endowed him with ideas and interests that brought into the open the conflicts within his party. His political experience offers an illuminating view of the nature of American politics at the end of the nineteenth century.

OSCAR HANDLIN

Contents

Contents

Bourbon Leader:
Grover Cleveland
and the
Democratic Party

I

The Young Lawyer

THE REVEREND RICHARD CLEVELAND seemed always on the move in the effort to escape poverty. Yet he never succeeded. There were always more offspring to feed and clothe; and the lovable preacher, although educated at Yale, was too prosaically dull in the pulpit to graduate beyond village charges.

Grover, fifth of his nine children, was born on June 18, 1837. The family then happened to be in Caldwell, New Jersey, but four years later it moved to Fayetteville, in western New York. There, and in nearby Clinton, the future President spent his early boyhood. Grover then gave no one any particular reason to prophesy that he was destined for great things. He was just another one of the boys of the town — healthy, rambunctiously energetic and wholesome. Intellectual and cultural pursuits failed to attract him, and he showed no special ability in the schoolroom.

Except for the one very positive influence of Presbyterian religious training within the family circle, Grover drifted through early boyhood. The daily prayers and the strict environment of a preacher's home provided him with a code that was to guide him during his entire life. This was good training as far as it went, and had the family plans for a college education materialized, Grover might well have acquired genuine intellectual and cultural depth and breadth.

Shortly after moving to Holland Patent, New York, the ailing Richard Cleveland died. Grover, then in his sixteenth year, was on his own, with no further hope of being sent to college. He faced the added responsibility of sharing the family expenses.

After spending a bleak year in New York City, where he and an older brother taught in the New York Institute for the Blind, Grover half-heartedly decided to seek his fortune in the West. En route, he visited his prosperous uncle, Lewis P. Allen, who lived near Buffalo. That ended the westward trek. It required but slight effort on his uncle's part to persuade the innately nonadventurous Grover to accept employment with him. There was a prospect then of admission to a Buffalo law firm where Grover could prepare himself for a legal career. Grover joined the Allen household on a farm where his uncle raised pedigreed cattle on a scale that made him nationally prominent. Allen had accumulated considerable wealth and prominence through real estate, banking and insurance ventures in and around Buffalo, where he had connections that made it possible for Grover, after a few months of keeping herd records on the farm, to enter a highly reputable Buffalo law firm as a clerk. Four years later he became a full-fledged attorney.

For twenty-six years, between 1855 and 1882, Grover remained in Buffalo, not venturing far outside the area for business or for pleasure. Twenty-five of those years constituted a continuation of his unconscious and unnoticed preparation for later conspicuous public service. Then suddenly he emerged into the limelight. In 1882, at the age of forty-four, he became Mayor of Buffalo; a year later he was Governor of New York, and two years later President of the United States.

The most significant aspect of this twenty-five-year period of preparation was its inadequacy. What he brought with him to Buffalo, more than his training and experience there, made it possible for him to rise to fame. Innate qualities, combined with his boyhood home training, carried him forward. His Buffalo years were important, chiefly because they contributed to his parochialism.

Buffalo, like so much of America, afforded opportunities for success in business and the professions; and Cleveland was one of those who managed to move smoothly and happily into and along the groove. He and the city seemed to have been made for each other. The boy was ambitious and hard working; Buffalo was ambitious and hard working. This gateway to the West, with its docks on the lake shore that hummed with activity, with its throbbing factories, with its bustling terminals serving four railroad lines, provided opportunity that fostered ambition. Measured by any standards, Grover could more than hold his own as a hard worker. He possessed phenomenal physical energy and power of concentration, at times working continuously for twenty-four hours without feeling tired.

The nature of his professional work reflected Cleveland's conservatism, lack of imagination and absence of an inner urge to become famous or wealthy. He avoided courtroom pleading and concentrated instead on legal

matters to be settled out of court. Judges often appointed
Cleveland to serve as a referee or arbitrator in cases that
showed a likelihood of settlement through agreement,
knowing that he was both willing and able to wade
through masses of material and apply a strictly letter-of-
the-law interpretation. His own clientele consisted largely
of companies requiring legal counsel in the Buffalo area.
Among these were the Buffalo, Rochester, and Pittsburgh
Railroad, the Lehigh Valley Railroad, the Standard Oil
Company and the Merchants' and Traders' Bank.

By the mid-1870's Cleveland had acquired a respectable
and moderately lucrative position in the Buffalo attorneys' guild. That seemed to be the limit of his professional
horizon, though now and then he showed interest in public office. Cleveland's reaction to an offer he received, in
1881, to be general counsel in western New York for the
New York Central Railroad was typical. The position
meant an addition to his moderate annual income of
$15,000. He had by then, however, saved about $75,000 and
had reached his economic goal, which seemed to him sufficient for his simple needs and wants. Hence he felt free
to weigh the offer in terms of his personal preferences.
Deciding that the work would interefere with his existing pleasant routine, keeping him at the beck and call of
an employer who would expect him to make trips outside
the Buffalo area, he independently refused the offer. By
so doing, in his later political career he escaped the charge
of having been a "railroadized" lawyer. His attitude toward corporations, however, was not unfriendly.

Comfortably at home in the city, Cleveland found himself also absorbing some of the less admirable tastes of
the Buffalo environment. Buffalo society was conspicu-

ously lacking in cultural and intellectual interests. Grover showed but little inclination to read anything beyond the call of duty — which meant his law books. Yet he had a liking for poetry, particularly for Tennyson. He memorized easily and years later quoted accurately. He never attended church, except while visiting his mother at Holland Patent, nor did he very long continue his initial close relationship with his uncle's family. He found the dignified, intellectual and cultural interests of the Allen family too dull; and in turn Mrs. Allen did not hesitate to make clear her disapproval of Grover's coarse friends.

Through these two decades, when Grover put aside his law books after a period of concentrated work, he habitually joined forces in a saloon with some rollicking, card-playing, boisterous pals. He liked to go with his friends on fishing or hunting excursions, or to clambakes or to the races. He took his fun almost exclusively in masculine company. As he acquired maturity, he became a member of the local Bar Association and of a number of clubs. In 1877 he helped found the City Club, and thereafter increasingly frequented its dining room rather than the saloons. He helped establish the sporty Beaver Island Club, dedicated to boating, fishing, swimming and duck shooting, with a clubhouse on the island it owned in the Niagara River. He felt no inclination to forswear his bachelor existence, although he did get involved in an affair which was later to cause him national political embarrassment.

Although the milieu of Buffalo did little to improve Grover's social habits, its provincial atmosphere imposed a far greater limitation upon his understanding of the economic-political world outside the boundaries of the city. Buffalo and Grover were so busy going upward for material or professional success and downward for recreation that there was no time to venture outward for understanding or inward for spiritual and philosophical contemplation. Buffalo was a gateway to the West, but its citizens rarely peered beyond the portals. The impact on Western farmers of the protective tariff, inadequate currency-credit facilities and monopolistic transportation systems received no more than casual notice in Buffalo. To Grover and his associates the problems of wage earners — unemployment, excessive hours of work and low pay — seemed unimportant. Areas outside Buffalo should and could of course, he thought, take care of themselves, just as Buffalo did. The Buffalo of his day was profiting both from the industrial revolution in the East and from being a terminal through which goods and people swarmed into and out of the dizzily expanding West. It took national depressions in its stride, as its population mounted from 42,000 in 1850 to over 81,000 in 1860 and to 155,000 in 1880. The good citizens contributed money and effort to aid sufferers when misfortune struck. Basically kind and sympathetic, Grover extended a helping hand to the needy, but even after he became a well-established lawyer his name never appeared on the published lists of subscribers to "causes" — such as the Buffalo Hospital or the Chicago fire sufferers. He never served on the board of trustees of a charitable institution or advocated charitable activity as a function of government.

The very narrowness of Cleveland's interests contributed not a little to his success. By concentrating on a few things, he was able to do those well on the strength of his industry, common sense and integrity. When confronted with a specific project as a practicing attorney or a public servant, Cleveland worked with a diligence that astounded persons not previously acquainted with his ways. Cleveland brought to his labor a great reserve of physical energy and a striking capacity to disregard discomfort. He was able to concentrate on each segment of a project without giving thought to the relative dullness or the relative importance of each item. He took it for granted that everything, large and small, was worthy of thorough study. In short, he was a plodder.

It was not his plodding, however, that most distinguished Cleveland among lawyers and later among political leaders, but rather his absolute integrity. Doubtless most lawyers and politicians were personally as honest, but many of them, swayed by the desire for power and money, often treated honesty as professionally expendable. Cleveland so exuded integrity that had he been more fastidious and less earthy in his social habits he would have seemed stuffy and self-righteous. Though his clear blue eyes and firm jaw gave the appearance of stern integrity, his burliness, his love of heavy food and taste for beer made him an approachable "good fellow."

A spirit of independence gave Cleveland great strength of character. From his boyhood onward he was irritated, rude and rebellious whenever his freedom was threatened. A mild and busy father had imposed on him only limited social restraints; and he suffered from few limitations in his life in Buffalo. The honesty with which he exercised this independence reflected his Calvinistic home training and was as conspicuous as his insistence on freedom. Perhaps it was fear of being trapped, of losing some of his independence, that so long kept him a bachelor.

It certainly appeared, in 1881, that Cleveland, the successful local attorney, intended to continue along his narrow, pleasant path. But during the very year that he had shied away from larger legal opportunities with the New York Central Railroad he was elected Mayor of Buffalo, thus stumbling into a political situation that led to his election to the Presidency of the United States three years later. That this should happen to him, of all people, must have astonished even the most avid Horatio Alger reader. No one could have been more surprised than Cleveland himself.

Cleveland's early political record had been undistinguished, unless honesty, conscientiousness and efficiency in local office were criteria for fame. He well demonstrated those qualities as a young Democratic ward worker, as Assistant District Attorney and as Sheriff of Buffalo County. This modest role in politics had begun in 1858, about the time when he was admitted to the bar. Two years earlier he had decided to be a Democrat. He later gave as his reason for this decision the greater moderation of the Democratic party and his distaste for the flamboyant, theatrical performance of Republican presidential candidate John C. Frémont, an opinion entirely consistent with his innate conservatism. Other factors, however, might well have influenced his decision. The members of the firm to which he was attached as a law clerk were ardent Democrats, as were the young men with whom he associated in the saloons and hotel lobbies and at sports events. On one occasion an argument over Democratic politics had ended in a well-attended, impromptu street fist fight between Cleveland and one Mike Falvey.

Cleveland began his political activity distributing campaign literature in his ward and watching the polls on election days. In 1863 he was elected ward supervisor — in a ward where he had a popular following among the German residents. Shortly thereafter he served briefly as Assistant District Attorney.

Cleveland's record during the Civil War was not conducive to political advancement. While others were profoundly moved by the crisis, he remained almost coldly calm. It may have been that he lacked the imagination to project his mind and emotions into the full meaning of the contest; possibly his innate conservatism and inherent independence caused him to resist a popular crusade. He was not a Copperhead, perhaps for the same reasons. It took imagination and daring to be a Copperhead — to envisage and to risk an acceptable termination of hostilities through negotiation rather than through complete military victory. Of least interest to Cleveland was the crusade against slavery. The plight of Negroes was far removed from his own life. His father had disapproved of abolitionism, and Grover's Maryland-born mother was not reared in an antislavery tradition.

With his characteristic independence Cleveland formed his own opinions on the crisis, irrespective of either partisan tactics or public sentiment. He was a War Democrat but with some reservations. He favored continuation of the war until preservation of the Union was assured, but he disagreed with the War Democrats who decried President Lincoln's "dictatorial," "unconstitutional" suspension of the writ of habeas corpus. Cleveland, unswayed by the vote-getting aspect of the Democratic position, stated to a friend that "the government has a right in time of war to resort to every possible method in order to protect itself." While he did not openly break with the War Democrats, he did, his family thought, vote for Lincoln in the 1864 election.

Cleveland's relative detachment caused him to feel no strong desire to enlist in the army. Instead, he assumed financial responsibility for his mother and sisters while his two brothers joined up. When he was subject to enlistment, in 1863, he hired a substitute for $150. Cleveland's feeling of responsibility to his mother and sisters was strong then, as always; his "martial spirit" was nil; and doubtless he did not consider the political advantage of a war record.

In 1870, at the age of thirty-two, Cleveland again sought and obtained political office. He was elected Sheriff of Buffalo County by a narrow margin. In seeking and even pulling wires to obtain that position, he was motivated purely by the economic security it would bring — about $40,000 from fees during the three-year term of office. He conducted the office efficiently and honestly and found the role rather pleasant. He felt at home with the coarse characters with whom he associated, he had plenty of leisure for hunting and fishing and time to fulfill his desire further to study law books, and his financial position steadily improved. He squirmed only twice when carrying out the responsibilities of this office — when he pressed the lever in the hanging of two convicts.

Upon the expiration of his term as Sheriff in 1873, Cleveland returned to his law practice, which he happily and successfully pursued until the mayoralty election in 1881. During these eight years he formed no special plans for the future, except that he did hope that his career as a lawyer would eventually carry him to the state Supreme Court bench. To his friends and associates he was just another respected practicing attorney. Then, of a sudden, a surprising chain of circumstances deposited him in the White House in less than four years.

I I
Rise to Power

PUBLIC indignation placed Grover Cleveland on the road to fame. Corruption and inefficiency had characterized the Buffalo city government for many years. Changes back and forth between the Democratic and Republican parties had made no difference. Politicians in both camps were equally bad, and certain scheming corruptionists had managed to make lucrative deals with the leaders of both parties. Finally a group of respected citizens, who paid substantial city tax bills, decided they could no longer afford the luxury of indifference to public affairs. Their sense of moral outrage was a seedbed for revolt. The same development had occurred in numerous cities since the early 1870's, most notably in New York City, where the conduct of the Tweed Ring had aroused a successful reform crusade. The New York City uprising brought fame to Democrat Samuel J. Tilden; the Buffalo uprising was to do the same for Cleveland.

The clique in control of the government, which happened to be Republican, failed to observe the danger. The 1880 Republican city convention nominated dubious characters for Mayor and for Comptroller. Immediately a large contingent of reputable Republicans protested loudly and convinced Democratic leaders of sufficient bipartisan support to assure victory if the latter would choose respectable candidates to head the ticket.

Reformers and practical politicians were really not asking for much. They sought an honest and courageous watchdog of the public coffers. They had no program of social service, slum clearance, health regulation, city beautification, civil service or city charter modernization. Their single-minded purpose was to save, not to spend, money. Even so, it was not easy to fill the vacancy. Eager Democratic party workers asked various leading businessmen to consider the nomination, for it was assumed that a businesslike administration should be conducted by a businessman. They were rebuffed at each approach. Everyone was too busy with his private affairs or would have to make too great a personal financial sacrifice if he took time off to be Mayor. Doubtless no one relished being dragged into the "dirty mess" involving unpleasant chores carried on with uncongenial political hacks and jobbers. When no businessman was found willing to serve, somebody thought of Cleveland, who reluctantly accepted.

During the ensuing campaign, Cleveland's statements were in complete agreement with the aims of the reformers — simply to eliminate the low morality and the high cost of the city government. "We believe," he said, "in the principle of economy of the people's money, and that when a man in office lays out a dollar in extravagance, he acts immorally by the people." He also announced that "public officials are the trustees of the people." He needed say no more. The ex-Sheriff was known to be honest and won by a comfortable majority.

His new post offered numerous opportunities to a reform-minded, politically ambitious man. He could count
on broad popular support for any action against the venal
corruptionists who for so long had been in command and
now had majority control of the city council. Moreover,
the slow-witted Aldermen played into the hands of the
new Mayor. All he had to do was to veto the corrupt
appropriation measures sent to him by the city council
and at the same time to state forthrightly his reasons
for the veto. Cleveland vetoed a five-year contract for
street cleaning to a company whose bid was over $100,000
more than the lowest bid of a competing concern. In so
doing he asserted that in his opinion the action of the
Aldermen was "the culmination of a most barefaced, im-
pudent, and shameless scheme to betray the interests of
the people, and to worse than squander the public
money." Public response was so vehement that the council was obliged to reverse its action.

Cleveland did not disappoint the solid citizens who
frowned upon government spending for city development,
but he did take action on the crying need for an adequate
city sewage outlet. Threats of lawsuits against the city
and the scandalous death rate from typhoid fever had
long since prepared the community to welcome a more
positive solution than the makeshift devices that previously had been tried and had failed. Cleveland proceeded
in his usual clearheaded and forthright manner. A board
of sewer commissioners received the necessary power and
money to construct the diversionary sewer recommended
by expert engineers. He showed himself to be an able
administrator when he recognized a specific need that
came within what he considered his rightful jurisdiction.

The new Mayor soon began to attract attention outside Buffalo, although not more than passing notice beyond the confines of western New York. He was one of a large number of mayors who were responding to widespread urban demand to clean up local governments and to eliminate the most obvious threats to health and to safety that had accompanied post-Civil War population growth and industrial development. Mayor Cleveland's program and achievements were very limited, superficial and almost incidental when compared with those of other reformers of the era. Much more notable was the record, for example, of Mayor Seth Low of Brooklyn, who dealt with such fundamentals as the unrealistic constitutional municipal-state relationship and the need for a merit civil service system. There was, nevertheless, something refreshing and arresting about Cleveland's crudely blunt vocabulary as he scolded the shameful and shameless majority on the Buffalo Board of Aldermen.

Cleveland was experiencing a recurrence of his earlier attacks of political ambition. Within six months after assuming office as Mayor, he was recruiting support for his governorship candidacy. In this first bid for high political office, Cleveland applied the formula that was to characterize his career for the rest of his life. It was as simple as it was self-contradicting: make no sordid deals involving the public purse strings; impress the voters with his independence of machine politics; quietly accept machine politics insofar as it was expedient. In short, be a politician without seeming to be one, and at the same time retain personal integrity. It was not a new formula, but few public men have been able to apply it with Grover Cleveland's startling success. In that success, however, it was not so much Cleveland's remarkable adeptness as the collection of circumstances that surrounded him. He was lucky — almost unbelievably lucky!

The public, as well as a large number of its leaders, was more than normally alert to and prepared to act against machine politics. The Tweed Ring excesses of the previous decade had quarantined Tammany Hall and had placed all politicians under strict observation for signs of machine-bossism. Cleveland, through his manner and his record, exuded so much independence that he was certain to attract at least favorable attention. His manner caught the eye of influential, brilliant and crusading Edgar K. Apgar of Albany, who was on the alert for new leadership in the state Democracy and who made it a point to comb the various state newspapers. Hence, in 1882, he came upon the account of Cleveland's street-cleaning contract veto. Soon Apgar was advertising Cleveland as a likely gubernatorial candidate.

Also advertising Cleveland's virtues was alert Charles W. McCune, who had important political advantages as editor of the Buffalo *Courier,* a member of the Democratic State Committee and one of the then somewhat politically clannish Irish-American citizenry. Another active pro-Clevelandite was David B. Hill. This youthful Mayor of Elmira hoped that he might ride into the lieutenant governorship on Cleveland's coattails. When these men and a few others mentioned the Buffalo Mayor as a possible candidate, they were asked: "Who in hell is Cleveland?" But they answered the question often enough to make their man noticed.

Cleveland and his promoters knew of course that organized support was imperative. Back in the 1860's and

1870's the Mayor had been active enough in Buffalo politics to understand and appreciate the practical side of the
profession. Cleveland had become Sheriff with the organized support of professionals. He knew, moreover, that
his elevation to the mayoralty was a political accident. He
realized that his only hope was to acquire a small core of
aggressive and loyal followers who would push him forward in the event that the convention looked for a compromise candidate.

Again fortune shone on Cleveland. The Democrats of
western New York resented having been so long by-passed
when the party selected its candidates for high offices.
Now, encouraged by Cleveland's cohorts, they saw their
chance to back Buffalo's Mayor for the governorship. At
the same time a handful of reform-minded party leaders
elsewhere discussed Cleveland as a possibility, and a few
of them, most notably the brilliant Apgar of Albany, became ardent champions of the burly western New Yorker.
Others gave him a passing thought in case it became
necessary to reach below the top shelf for a candidate.

Luckily for Cleveland the top shelf was then sadly
depleted, and the two most important anti-Tammany
groups, which normally would be expected to unite on a
candidate, had failed to agree on the matter. The Tilden-
Manning wing of the party, headed by the powerful and
able state chairman Daniel Manning, had, at least tenta-
tively, lined up behind General Henry W. Slocum of
Brooklyn. The other reform organization, the County
Democracy, which embraced such able New York City
leaders as Abram S. Hewitt and William C. Whitney,
was adamantly anti-Slocum. It suspected Slocum of being
secretly friendly to Tammany, involved in frauds and of

mediocre ability. The only other candidate with substantial backing, Roswell P. Flower, was handicapped by personal mediocrity, by having alienated Manning and by
having bid for Tammany support.

Cleveland resolved to keep his initial advantage of freedom from any alliance with either of the warring factions. A month before the state convention was to con-
vene, the impatient Apgar urged Cleveland to pay a visit
to chairman Manning, but the more deliberate Buffalo
Mayor, after much consideration, vetoed the proposal,
contending that if knowledge of it leaked to the public
the visit might be held against him as evidence that he
was not "free from any alliance." Finally, however, a few
days before the convention opened, Cleveland surrepti-
tiously made some quick sorties from behind his ostenta-
tious camouflage of aloofness from machine politics. He
told certain of his loyal workers, including his close friend
and law partner Wilson S. Bissell, what to do at the convention. Two of them were to "go the first thing to Daniel Manning and urge with the utmost vehemence my
nomination. Never mind what he says — pound away."
Cleveland followed this up by a brief on-the-scene appearance. His cohorts had urged him to do this in response to the expressed interest of several delegates to get
a look at and meet this newcomer to state politics. The
day before the balloting began he therefore spent a
few hours in Syracuse, where he held a shirt-sleeve levee
in a hotel lobby and, more significantly, called upon the
mighty Manning.

Meanwhile, luck continued to work for Cleveland. A
few hours after the convention delegates arrived, news
reached them of an event that automatically enhanced

Cleveland's chances. The Republican gubernatorial candidate would not be able Governor Alonzo B. Cornell, but Charles J. Folger, whose candidacy was forced upon the convention by the machine tactics of Chester A. Arthur, Roscoe Conkling and Jay Gould. This news stimulated antimachine sentiment and fostered victory-at-the-polls optimism in the Democratic camp. In such an atmosphere, Cleveland's reputation for forthright independence stood him in good stead.

Before the balloting began, Whitney, spokesman for the County Democracy, called on Manning in his room. Walking up to the upstate boss, who was conferring with a burly man, Whitney blurted out to Manning: "The man who can defeat the Republicans worst is that buxom Buffalonian, Grover Cleveland. You up-State Democrats want to unite with the New York Democracy on Cleveland, and we'll not only elect him Governor this Fall but President a little later. I have never met him but I know he's all right." Manning thereupon smilingly introduced his companion, Grover Cleveland. The result was victory for Cleveland on an early ballot.

Cleveland's victory at the convention assured him the governorship. The widespread public anger against bossism was so intense and the contrast between the Republican and Democratic response was so obvious that the final outcome was a foregone conclusion. Public distaste for anything that smacked of Jay Gould's influence in politics was equaled only by the unpopularity of Tammany Hall. Whereas the Republican party leadership had surrendered to Gould, the Democratic party leadership had not only ignored Tammany wishes but had gone so far as to nominate a man independent of all political bosses, machines and factions and but vaguely identified with any organized group. Even his connection with the Democratic party seemed to be accidental and incidental. Cleveland appeared to be a nonpolitical, disinterested citizen-crusader for honest government whom Buffalo Democrats and Republicans alike had supported to clean the administration of their city affairs.

In the election campaign that followed, Cleveland acted the Olympian, as he was to do during all his future campaigns. There was nothing original in this; in fact, it was a concept of an earlier day that continued to be used successfully from time to time. It certainly was the wisest course for Cleveland, placing him above the level of active, conspicuous political activity at a time when hosts of voters were cynically, almost sadistically, condemning politicians in general. The voters were left to speculate on the degree to which the candidate himself condoned or inspired the political maneuvers of his vote-seeking supporters. In their state of frustration many confused, uneasy voters were easily led to accept the naïve rationalization that politicians were bad, but that some candidates for political office were not really politicians.

In this particular campaign it was wise for Cleveland to remain aloof for still another important reason. If he wandered far beyond the outskirts of Buffalo, he might well say the wrong things to party workers, to local dignitaries and to public audiences because he was woefully unacquainted with outside people, places and issues. Hence he remained in the background, leaving the planning and the conduct of the campaign to the astute Manning.

It was so obvious that the Democrats would win that it

was impossible for either the politicians or the public to feel excited. Democratic leaders were nevertheless so anxious to win that they did not hesitate to water down the reform aspect of their crusade by placating Tammany Hall. When confronted with an opportunity to unite with a citizens' committee on reformer Allan Campbell for Mayor of New York City, the County Democracy, led by Whitney, bowed to the objections of Tammany and formed a compromise slate. But no one connected this deal with Cleveland in faraway Buffalo. Many Republicans joined with the Democrats to register their disgust with the raw tactics employed by manipulators in the selection of the Republican candidate. Grover Cleveland won the election by a tremendous plurality.

I I I

The Governorship

CLEVELAND approached his new position with a determination to be successful. On the morning after the election he felt "as if it were time to write to someone who will believe what I write," and to his brother, the Reverend William N. Cleveland, he confessed his doubts as to whether he could "well perform" his duties "in such a manner as to do some good to the people of the state. I know there is room for it, and I know that I am honest and sincere in that desire to do well, but the question is whether I know enough to accomplish what I desire." He would have felt "so much safer" if his mother were alive, he admitted, because he had "always thought that her prayers had so much to do with my success."

Cleveland had no grandiose dreams of the future, either for himself or for the State of New York. He did not view the governorship as a steppingstone to personal political advancement. He meant it when he wrote to his brother: "I have no idea of re-election or any higher political preferment . . . but [will] be very thankful if I can well serve one term as the people's governor."

Cleveland's conception of what a "people's governor" should be was limited and essentially negative. He stanchly believed that the Governor's primary duty was to conduct his office with complete honesty and economy, and he often roared like a lion when he saw violations of these simple virtues. He had a strong sense of his own and of other people's prerogatives, and he was known to roar with equal vehemence when he thought these prerogatives were endangered.

Had Cleveland entertained a broader and more positive conception of government in general, he might have become either a truly great leader or an utter failure. But he thought that a governor had no right to force his will upon the legislature and furthermore that no branch of the government could interfere, beyond the very minimum of absolute necessity, with the economic and social privileges of individuals and of business. Having thereby limited the circle of his endeavors, he was always on safe ground when he struck out at violators of long-established and cherished rights. Furthermore he operated in a period of relative stability, when the public was not clamoring for change.

Cleveland's negativism was especially striking in the realm of social legislation. His mind was remarkably unreceptive to new ideas. While evidences of outright dishonesty and of cynicism in political practices disturbed a growing number of citizens, there was also an undercurrent of demand for governmental action designed to give more direct economic and social protection to the people. Many felt that the government aided businessmen, yet allowed those businessmen to exploit the laborers, farmers and consumers. In the 1880's the state legislature began to feel the impact of that demand. In New York City and in other industrial areas direct pressure for extended governmental action came mostly from urban workers. Low wages, high prices and rents, sweatshops and on-the-job accidents generated unrest and ultimately organized action.

Such deplorable conditions were not new, but they were made much worse by the rapid industrial growth, with its accompanying development of monopolistic business combinations, recurring economic depressions, labor-saving machinery and the flood of competing immigrant workers. Though hardship was widespread, it was especially conspicuous in New York City, the nation's largest industrial center. In 1876 a committee of workingmen had in desperation called upon the Mayor for unemployment relief. He curtly informed them that it was not an obligation of government to furnish jobs. In 1882, the year of Cleveland's election to the governorship, another depression began. At its height, one third to one half of the factories of the entire state were closed.

The workingmen organized. They made New York City the birthplace of the modern labor movement. In 1883 there were about one hundred trade unions in the city, embracing a hundred thousand members, and there was a corresponding growth of unionization elsewhere in the state. In addition to strikes and boycotts, the unions used politics as an instrument. In 1880 the Workingmen's Assembly, a state organization of labor unions, brought about the election of twenty men to the legislature and effectively used blackball tactics against unfavorable candidates.

Protest translated into political action also came from

persons, such as Assemblyman Theodore Roosevelt, who were in no way connected with organized labor and indeed were often vehemently against unions in sentiment. These protesters championed public resentment against the highhanded, monopolistic, unscrupulous practices of certain employers. The result was political action, although limited in scope, to further governmental regulation of specific business activities.

Cleveland viewed social legislation as heretically bad. He favored limited regulation of certain types of private enterprises that were creatures of government through charters, but he opposed any action that might interfere with an individual's freedom of contract. He thus defended the prevailing view of the proper role of the individual, of business and of the government.

Cleveland's most dramatic action early in his term was the veto of the Five Cent Fare bill, a measure to reduce the fare on the New York City elevated railroad. The current rate was five cents, except during rush hours when workers returned to their homes. Then it was ten cents. The company could well afford the lower fare at all hours, for even with its stock watered to twice the investment it was earning substantial profits. This fact and the knowledge that the much-despised Jay Gould controlled the company for his own ends created great popular sentiment for the bill. A respectable body of supporters felt that Gould, in combining two companies into one monopolistic concern, had clearly violated an implied contract as to service requirements, had concealed profits, and had thereby forfeited the privileges of the original charters. This trickery was considered loophole enough to warrant immediate legislative reform action.

Gould could then seek redress from the courts, if he chose. But that action would compel him to open his books to show whether the charges of trickery in hiding some of the profits were valid.

Support for the Five Cent Fare bill came from a wide segment of the public, from most newspapers, from many prominent figures and from Tammany Hall. The bill had passed in the legislature with little more than a murmur of dissent.

Cleveland's veto in reckless disregard of public opinion was unexpected. His demeanor added still more to the surprise of his action. This burly Governor returned the bill with a veto message so lacking in guile, so uncompromising, so scolding in tenor, and so obviously the product of his own thought that it had a disarming effect. He stated in his message that the measure was clearly unconstitutional, violating the right of contract protected by the first article of the federal Constitution. The bill was morally and legally wrong, because investors had been encouraged to enter into the risky elevated railway venture by the promise, prescribed by law, of liberal fares. It would be wrong to reduce the rate without a careful examination of the exact return on the investment. Under existing railway law the state had the legal right to make reductions if the returns were above ten per cent, but only after examination of the company's financial position. Cleveland also left the distinct impression that he believed the measure was motivated by vindictiveness and prejudice. He thus had sound legal grounds for vetoing the bill, and unlike almost everyone else involved in the matter he was unwilling to leave the responsibility for decision to the courts.

While the popular enthusiasm for the bill reflected an angry groping for justice on the part of an aroused people, the response to the scolding in Cleveland's message was a frustrated, uneasy retreat into conservatism. The people had been spanked; and they reacted like children who knew they were wrong. Such newspapers as the New York *Times* and the New York *Sun,* which had previously supported the bill, now agreed that the veto was legally sound. Theodore Roosevelt contritely stated that he too had been wrong in voting for the measure in the legislature. In due course the legislature decisively sustained the veto.

The drama had deeper meaning and portent than was involved in the mere fate of the bill. Cleveland's uncompromising defense of the letter of the law, his completely literal interpretation of the Constitution, added to his popularity among men whose chief concern was freedom from governmental restraint. And Cleveland's personal triumph defined a technique he was to use over and over again. The course was "safe and sound," both economically and politically. With monotonous consistency during his entire public career, Cleveland reacted in the same way, with a few grudgingly executed exceptions and occasional variations in details. His approach was that of a narrow legalist rather than that of a pioneering public servant.

A factor that often afforded Cleveland an excuse to reject bills on legal grounds was the frequency with which they came to him in slipshod form. He methodically waded through the wordage of bills, looking for errors and contradictions. He found many, and he almost invariably returned the bills containing them to the

legislature with brusque messages. Cleveland often returned bills for corrections and then signed them. During
his second year in office, while he was earnestly and
courageously supporting Roosevelt's municipal and
county reform efforts, he still yielded to his legalistic
obsession. Roosevelt, irritated with Cleveland's veto of
the final bill in the series on what seemed to be the flimsy
excuse of "trifling verbal inaccuracies," recalled that "the
Governor had previously returned six of the other municipal reform measures for verbal correction; but as it
turned out, most of the errors to which he called attention were in those portions of the bills which merely
recited, without change or amendment, the original law
which had been on the statute book for years, and with
which our measures had really nothing to do. I therefore
had them returned to the Governor forthwith, four of
them without change, and the others with slight and unimportant verbal alterations." If Cleveland favored the
purpose of a bill, however, and found its legal errors not
too flagrantly offensive, he sometimes signed it. This
happened often enough to indicate that part of his obsession with legal hairsplitting was based on a desire to
find an excuse to kill a measure. He was able to maintain
this practice because legislative bodies continued to operate chaotically.

Although deficiencies in bills gave Cleveland an excuse
for vetoing them, he did not take the opportunity to go on
to positive recommendations. Justifiable as many of his
vetoes may have been, the purposes of some of the bills
were nevertheless worthy. Rarely, if ever, did Cleveland
write a veto message of a truly positive nature. He sometimes included a grudging recognition that a situation

required remedy, but he did not plead for action. He was more instructive than constructive, pointing out technical weaknesses in a bill without using his position to inspire public or legislative opinion to make necessary changes. This reticence was due to his extreme reluctance to participate in the legislative function and to accept governmental interference as a proper remedy for an unsatisfactory situation. The Five Cent Fare bill was characteristic. In his veto Cleveland had failed to emphasize the imperative need for bringing the Gould railway company to task.

Typical of Cleveland's attitude on labor legislation was his veto early in 1884 of a maximum hours law for the conductors and drivers of horse-drawn streetcars who had been working fourteen and sixteen hours a day. The bill limited their workday to twelve hours, but it had been amended by the time it reached the Governor to permit longer hours of work for extra compensation. Cleveland flatly vetoed it. He said it interfered with the employers' and employees' right of contract and was "class legislation."

A notable exception to Cleveland's opposition to labor legislation was a measure to abolish cigar making in tenement houses. The bill was supported by Assemblyman Theodore Roosevelt, then equally hostile to labor unions. A personal tour of the scene of operations had shocked the legislator. Upset by the unhealthy and sordid living and working conditions, he personally urged the Governor to sign the bill, which Cleveland reluctantly did. Roosevelt's influence was undoubtedly significant, for Cleveland was well aware of the Assemblyman's more usual antipathy toward labor legislation.

There were, however, substantial differences between

the two men. The solid Cleveland on rare occasions made grudging concession to new views; the meteoric Roosevelt gradually accepted them and became their champion. Thus Roosevelt was angry when the New York Court of Appeals, in the celebrated Jacobs case, declared the cigar makers' law unconstitutional. "It was this case," he later said, "which first waked me to a dim and partial understanding of the fact that the courts were not necessarily the best judges of what should be done to better social and industrial conditions." To Cleveland such thoughts were heresy. Cleveland and Roosevelt also differed in their views on philanthropy. The former showed no interest in either private or governmental charity; the latter, trained to an aristocratic creed of stewardship, had less difficulty in accepting the idea that the state sometimes needed to be paternalistic.

Cleveland, like the majority of his constituents, was more receptive to the crusade for "good government" than to the pressures for social legislation. As Governor he became identified with the "good government" element mainly through his appointive power and his cooperation with reform-minded legislators like Roosevelt. In his determination to get worthy officeholders Cleveland studied the qualifications of prospective appointees, and no office was so minor as to be awarded on the mere recommendation of an associate. It was very much in character when Cleveland rewarded a political ally by signing a bill to eliminate the use of his newspaper for state advertising.

Inevitably Cleveland ran afoul of Tammany Hall. "Honest John" Kelly, Tammany boss, was ambitious to augment his power through patronage and favors. He had been leader since shortly after Tweed's defeat in

1871 and had rebuilt the Hall into a smoothly operating organization, free of theft or scandal, applying "business-like" methods to its functions — patronage, elective offices, direct aid to the needy, intercession with authorities when persons were in trouble with hoodlums and police, and entertainment for citizens and their children.

When Cleveland became Governor, there was relative serenity in the Democratic camp. Tammany had not only acquiesced in his nomination but had jumped on his band wagon when it became apparent he would capture the prize. Election results had shown that Kelly had cooperated with the upstate machine and its gubernatorial candidate. The upstate Democrat responded to Kelly's good behavior and to the practical fact of Tammany's power on election days by showing a willingness to relax the Tiger's probationary status. Then in the spring of 1883, four months after he assumed office, the new Governor inadvertently stepped on the tail of the Tammany Tiger.

Cleveland had not made any concessions to Tammany, yet the Tammany legislators had cooperated with him in passing measures to reorganize the immigration department and the harbor masters. They clearly expected that a portion of the patronage involved would go to their organization. There were also several other jobs to be filled, and Kelly and his henchmen began to mutter ominously over their failure to receive a single crumb. Those mutterings became louder when Cleveland nominated ex-State Senator William H. Murtha, an associate of boss McLaughlin's rival Brooklyn machine, to the position of Immigration Commissioner.

Tammany's response was instantaneous. On order from

Kelly, the Tammany legislators in the Senate joined with delighted Republican colleagues in a successful move to refer the nomination to a committee. But Kelly made clear to Cleveland that if some other jobs went to Tammany and if Murtha promised Tammany a share of the two hundred subordinate positions at his disposal, Kelly would withdraw his opposition.

Kelly waited; Cleveland waited. On May 4, the last day before the legislature adjourned, Tammany senatorial spokesman Thomas F. Grady wrote the Governor requesting "as a special favor" the appointment of former Alderman Bryan Reilly as a harbor master. "I hope," begged Grady, "that you will kindly make the appointment for me, as it will place me in a most humiliating position with my people here if, with eleven appointments to be made, I should fail to secure one of them for so good a man as Mr. Reilly." That same day, almost as if in reply to this plea, Cleveland submitted a long list of nominations to the Senate, not one of which went to a Tammany man. Someone later remarked: "Out of all the three hundred places . . . Tammany was not guaranteed so much as a night watchman at Castle Garden." Tammany's response was again to unite with the Republicans in a successful move to block confirmation of all the nominations. Thereupon the incensed Cleveland, apparently having naïvely expected capitulation, angrily said to Daniel Lamont, his secretary: "Give me a sheet of paper. I'll tell the people what a set of d —— d rascals they have upstairs!"

In Cleveland's blistering message to the Senate he described the supposed virtues of Murtha — his integrity, benevolence and experience. The Senate action on Murtha, he said, "is not based upon any allegation of unfitness," but rather "has its rise in an overweening greed for patronage." When the clerk finished reading the message to the Senate, the infuriated Grady jumped to his feet and made a speech in which he asserted that the Murtha nomination was partisan in character and that the Governor's message was an "insult to the dignity of a legislative body." He thereupon moved that the message be referred to the Committee on Grievances. In the confusion the motion never reached the voting stage, nor did the message. The Senate adjourned *sine die,* without confirming Cleveland's nominees.

The politically inexperienced, impulsive, independent, prerogative-conscious Governor had stubbed his toe, but as he pitched forward he landed on higher ground in the opinion of the general public. He had indignantly, righteously, indomitably refused to retreat before the nefarious Tammany Tiger and had defended his constitutional right to choose nominees for appointive offices independently. In the public view, Cleveland had acted with refreshing moral correctness.

Yet in doing so he had failed to launch a crusade against machine politics as such and had endangered the constructive program of the party. Without the cooperation of Tammany, the Democrats were impotent in the legislature and seemed destined to lose strength in the next election. By alienating Tammany, Cleveland had freed it from the restraining influence of experienced, pragmatic state chairman Manning.

Cleveland's action destroyed the possibility of implementing two valuable reforms. In the case of the harbor masters' bill the New York City department of docks adequately carried out the necessary minimum functions, but the immigration service remained in the hands of the exploitive, dishonest and inefficient board that the new legislation had intended to replace.

At first Cleveland entertained the notion of calling an extra session of the legislature to implement the new harbor masters' and immigration agencies, but cooler heads prevailed upon him to drop the idea. Kelly and his cohorts were willing to allow the storm to subside. Grady, two days after the adjournment of the legislature, told a news reporter: "This whole matter is a tempest in a teapot. . . . Governor Cleveland and I are the best of friends. . . . So far as I know there are no personal feelings between us which are not of the most cordial character." Soon Cleveland left Albany for a vacation — doubtless to the great relief of unity-promoter Manning.

The state Democratic convention was held in September. A complete Manning slate was nominated, without objection from Tammany. Boss Kelly recognized that Cleveland's action had sprung from political inexperience and saw the primary importance of party unity. Cleveland did not attend the convention.

The Governor, meanwhile, had great fun hunting and fishing with his old cronies and rollicking with them in the Dutchman's Tavern in Buffalo. Yet his ruffled temper was not calmed, nor did he display a spirit of forgiveness toward Tammany. His sense of grievance was too deeply imbedded. He was disturbed when he heard that Kelly planned to seek the re-election of Grady to the Senate, as a reward for loyal services. But the gifted orator Grady had alienated many of his constituents as his proclivity for wine, women and song had led him into a life of

outright debauchery. Furthermore, his action in the legislature that killed the immigration reform measure designed to end the scandalous exploitation of newcomers
was too much for the God-fearing Irish voters of his district. Kelly soon discovered the cause was lost, and Grady
eventually withdrew.

But Cleveland did not wait, nor did he consult friends
and political leaders on the matter. He wrote and sent to
Honest John Kelly a letter insisting "that Mr. Grady
should not be returned to the next Senate." Bluntly he
stated that his own "personal comfort and satisfaction"
were involved, but went on to insist "that good legislation,
based upon a pure desire to promote the interests of the
people and the improvement of legislative methods, are
also deeply involved." He went on to conclude: "I for-
bear to write in detail of the other considerations having
relation to the welfare of the party and the approval to be
secured by a change for the better in the character of its
representatives. These things will occur to you without
suggestion from me."

Kelly did not reveal the letter to the public until after
his efforts to renominate Grady seemed doomed to failure,
which put him in the embarrassing position of being unable to function as a complete boss. Apparently in an
effort to fix the blame on Cleveland and to save his own
face, he made the Governor's letter public. Thereupon
began a bitter, open fight between Cleveland and Tammany. To the politicians Cleveland's action was gross
folly. He had defied two truisms of American politics,
namely that, barring near miracles, the Democrats could
not carry New York State without the aid of Tammany,
and that the Democrats could not carry a presidential

election without New York State's large electoral vote. The normal election in the state was decided by a margin of about 25,000 with Tammany voters included in the Democratic column. Of these Kelly could deliver, as he saw fit, a solid block of 60,000. Everybody knew that he had delivered in the past, and he might again deliver, this block to the Republicans. With Cleveland deliberately goading the vindictive Kelly, nothing seemed left of the long, patient efforts of Manning and others to complete the slow-healing wounds in the Democratic party.

There was moral justification for Cleveland's action, yet again he had pointed up his loyalty to the cause of "good government," without any indication of just how bossism would be "swept away." Even to approach that end called for a constructive social and civil service program that would permit the government to replace the services performed by the boss-dominated machines. Such developments, however, were completely foreign to the Cleveland mind and temperament. It would remain for later generations of leaders, more educated, more imaginative and more flexible, to make sound beginnings on that complex problem.

During the election campaign Cleveland did urge business leaders to exert more effort to place men representing their interests in the state legislature. He offered this suggestion at a banquet of the Chamber of Commerce in New York City: "Is there care taken to have champions of this all-important interest in the halls of the Legislature? And is it there distinctly enough represented?" He warned his listeners to bear in mind that while they "may labor and toil, in the whirl and excitement of business, to build new warehouses and to add to the city's wealth and to your own," at the same time "ignorant, negligent men among your lawmakers can easily and stealthily pull down." This slap at Tammany was most certainly an expression of sympathy for the businessman. Whether his hearers were moved most by the anti-Tammany or by the probusiness implications of those remarks was not clear, but that they were pleased was abundantly apparent.

One tangible outcome of the Cleveland-Kelly bout was the decline in Democratic votes. The election results placed the legislature in the hands of the Republicans, while all but one of the state offices went to the Democrats. The Democratic victories, however, were by a very narrow over-all 17,000 plurality, in comparison with Cleveland's 200,000 of the previous year. The election outcome had a distinctly sobering effect on Cleveland and on state Democratic party leader Manning. Cleveland's re-election a year later could not be considered a foregone conclusion. Although previously Cleveland had blocked off from his mind the consideration of political expediency, the election results must have jolted him into an acute awareness that he faced possible defeat as a reward for his brashness. Pride, resentment against his persecutors and ambition aroused by the experience of having tasted the fruit of power now stirred in him. He became more calculating and more cautious. This change pleased and relieved Manning. The two men now began to work in closer alliance, and Cleveland consulted more frequently with Whitney, influential member of the County Democracy.

It was as if Cleveland had acquired a new pair of eyeglasses. They gave him longer but not broader or deeper vision. He continued to view the demands of organized labor and the call for social legislation of any sort as outside the proper role of government and as violations of the individual freedom and property rights guaranteed by the Constitution. But he now saw more clearly the danger of running afoul of certain Democratic factions. That did not mean, however, that he completely placed himself under the direction of the professional politicians. He continued to be unfriendly toward Tammany. Now that the legislature was definitely in the hands of the Republicans, he no longer faced the politically dangerous possibility of having to deal with a legislature in which Tammany forces held the balance of power, and he could also nobly identify himself with the cause of "good government" by association with the coterie of Republican reformers led by Theodore Roosevelt. It was in his reception of Roosevelt's reform acts that the new Cleveland was most revealed.

As chairman of the important City Committee, Roosevelt brought about a series of legislative committee investigations that exposed shockingly corrupt and wasteful practices in certain departments of the City and County of New York. He then pushed to passage some useful measures to correct the evils. Cleveland unhesitatingly signed all but one of them into law, disregarding Tammany's involvement in the reform. The blunt manner in which he ignored the complaints of aggrieved professional politicians and proclaimed the virtues of the bills as he signed them won for Cleveland the plaudits of many. He was doubtless pleased when a *Puck* cartoon depicted Cleveland and Roosevelt arm in arm, surveying a totally exhausted, dejected Tammany Tiger, with its teeth and claws scattered on the floor about him. Shortly before that a cartoon had represented Roosevelt clipping the Tiger's claws all by himself.

Soon, however, it was remarked of Cleveland that "good government" crusader George W. Curtis "knows now that his idol has clay feet." This remark grew out of Cleveland's refusal to cooperate with Roosevelt when the young legislator attacked the non-Tammany Democracy. Two episodes gave rise to this condemnation of Cleveland. Roosevelt's committee, after a lengthy investigation of Sheriff Alexander V. Davidson, charged that on six counts the Sheriff had demonstrated gross misconduct in office. Roosevelt and the independent press felt that Davidson should be dismissed from office. Cleveland did not act, nor did he offer reasons for his failure to do so. This aroused suspicion, for Sheriff Davidson was the leader of Irving Hall, similar to Tammany Hall, but with the important difference that Davidson was friendly toward Manning and Cleveland.

The second event was Cleveland's veto of Roosevelt's Tenure of Office bill, aimed at ridding the New York City government of Hubert O. Thompson, whose wasteful and corrupt conduct as Commissioner of Public Works had aroused the indignation of the public and press, regardless of party affiliation. The Democratic *Times* believed that "facts enough have been brought out to stamp his record with inefficiency, extravagance, and corruption second only to that of one of his predecessors in office named Tweed." The bill authorized the next Mayor to appoint a new Commissioner of Public Works before the present incumbent's term expired. Cleveland vetoed the measure eight days before the end of the legislative session on the ground that it was so slipshod in language that it would certainly result in a hopeless tangle for the next Mayor. He said it was the most careless legislation ever sent to him. Disappointed champions of reform argued that the defects were minor and could have been remedied by the next session of the legislature or left to the courts. Most reformers, however, were less interested in the disposition of the bill than in speculation over what really motivated Cleveland's action.

There indeed was room aplenty for speculation. Cleveland's failure to dismiss Sheriff Davidson and his rescue of Commissioner Thompson evaded a serious disruption in the non-Tammany segment of the party. Neither Davidson nor Thompson had the confidence of the public, but they did have power in the all-important gatherings that selected delegates to conventions. There was no question that Cleveland had become increasingly delegate-conscious, as Democratic cohorts pointed out to him that residence at the White House was a possibility he should not overlook.

Roosevelt and the many others who decried the veto believed that Cleveland's action was a result not only of his legalistic background but also of his political ambition. They did not hesitate with varying degrees of intensity to emphasize the political aspect of his retreat from reform. The most generous and most logical interpretation of the Governor's failure to remove Sheriff Davidson and Commissioner Thompson was simply that Cleveland had finally emerged as a hard-hitting, realistic, ambitious politician. The contrast between his politically reckless onslaught against Kelly and Tammany on the one hand and his negativeness regarding Davidson and Thompson on the other was striking evidence that experience and ambition had moderated his zeal for righteousness. Unlike most men in high elective office, Cleveland had arrived in the governorship without consuming political ambition. Now the effects of ambition upon his future course of action remained to be seen.

As the 1884 legislative session ended, in mid-May, Cleveland's position in New York politics was far from secure. Unless he left the possibility of re-election to the governorship in 1885 to mere chance, he would need to do some careful fence building. His alienation of Tammany had created a hole in the state Democracy that indicated almost certain defeat unless he took positive action. He needed to make up his mind to either control his personal inclinations and seek a *modus vivendi* with Tammany, or launch a "citizens' crusade" that would enlist substantial voter support from independent and Republican ranks. While he seemed to waver, the winds of chance were gathering for a storm that might blow him either back to his cluttered rooming house in Buffalo or into the White House.

I V

Presidential Candidate

In june, 1884, it became clear that Cleveland was almost certain to receive the nomination for the Presidency. That month Tilden and Manning, the two most influential men in the national Democratic party, decided it should be so; and with the exception of the Tammany Tiger nothing on the political horizon appeared to stand in their way. Their voices carried far, for they spoke from the summit of an imposing political structure in the national Democratic party organization.

This structure had been erected by the Bourbon Democrats, who were the conservative spokesmen of business in the party. Their function was to prevent control of the government by farmers, wage earners and inefficient, irresponsible, corrupt officeholders. The Bourbons believed governmental interference with the natural laws of economics imposed a check on progress and thus government regulation and government aid should be limited to the barest necessity. Because taxation was a drag on the economy, it was to be kept to a minimum. Hence the managers of the public purse must be efficient, economical, honest; opposed to spending money for paternalism and special privilege.

The protective tariff, which interfered with natural law and was a subsidy to special interests, violated Bourbon doctrine. Most protariff manufacturers were therefore Republicans, and most antitariff railroad operators, bankers and merchants were Bourbon Democrats. Expediency sometimes caused an individual Bourbon Democrat to deviate from the cause of limited government, but if he ever did so to meet farmer or wage-earner demands, he was placed on strict probation by the Bourbon hierarchy. He was allowed nevertheless to have friendly relations with the business-minded Republican leadership.

The Bourbon group had come into existence as a cohesive political force at the end of the crucial national convention of 1868. At that conclave, a coalition of Bourbons had defeated the spokesmen of distraught Western and Southern farmers. Through the next three decades the conservatives uncompromisingly and successfully suppressed agrarian and labor discontent. In consequence the Democratic party missed many opportunities to overcome the superior voting strength of the Republican party. The Bourbons, many of them intimately connected with railroads, did not shrink from defeat at the polls in order to retain control of the party machinery. They often prevented popular agrarian and labor reformers from becoming delegates to conventions. Consequently there were many Bourbon delegates at national party conclaves who were devoted allies of the Tilden-Manning New York organization.

Tilden-Manning power was the product of the voting strength of the New York Democracy at conventions and at the polls and of the personal prestige of Tilden and the political skill of Manning. The austere Tilden was respectable, wealthy, brilliant, popular with the public and revered by his allies. In 1868 he had been one of the chief architects of the national Bourbon Democracy, in due course furnishing the party and himself with a much-needed formula for votes — "good government" reform.

Tilden's emergence as a reformer was ironical. As a practical politician he had earlier accepted the traditional practice of dividing New York party control between the respectable state-national leaders and corrupt Tammany Hall. Though Tilden had been a member of Tammany, he had not attempted to rule it, recognizing the exclusive prerogative of William Marcy Tweed and his Ring. Tweed had shown equal restraint in state and national party affairs, the bailiwick of Tilden and of the Regency. But in 1868 the greedy Tweed bid for control of the state party and thereby ran afoul of its chairman Tilden. Tweed won the first rounds, but the desperate and relentless Tilden took advantage of Tammany vulnerability to defeat Tweed in the 1871 election. Intra-Tammany fighting between nationality groups and defections in the top leadership clique contributed to this outcome. But a more important factor was the public outrage as it became known that the Tweed Ring, from 1868 to 1871, had stolen over one hundred million dollars.

Tilden, once known as the Great Forecloser because of his hardheaded business activity, now came to be called the Great Reformer. As a political reformer, and at the same time as an economic conservative, he now became an officeholder. In 1875 he was elected to the governorship and next year he became the Democratic presidential nominee. His position as reformer, however, did not impel him to destroy the partnership with the city machine. Although he ruined Tweed, Tilden made no attempt to destroy Tammany itself or even to frighten it with a crusade for a civil service system.

To his luster as a reformer and his reputation as a skillful politician, he added the popularity of a martyr. It was widely believed that the election of 1876 had robbed him of the Presidency. In 1884, despite a paralytic stroke that left him a tottering old man who could not speak above a whisper, he was still politically powerful. Many worshipful Democrats could not bring themselves to accept the fact that Tilden could not be their 1884 standard-bearer; others waited uneasily for his word to that effect and for his choice for the nomination.

Most politicians knew that by watching the movements of Manning they could learn what Tilden was willing to accept. Manning, deeply loyal, had taken over much of the responsibility of directing the Bourbon Democracy as Tilden became less active. In 1882 he became chairman of the state committee and in 1884 was the acknowledged custodian of Tilden's power and the manager of a political organization with great state and national power. He would have much to say about the presidential nomination.

When Manning, after consultation with Tilden, made it clear to all that the gate was open for Cleveland, the burly Governor was already standing hesitatingly and awkwardly halfway down the path. Tilden and Manning certainly had compelling reasons to welcome Cleveland's candidacy. But there were also factors that made them reluctant. They were concerned and irritated by Cleveland's lack of political and intellectual sophistication. Their own intellects were superior and their interests more catholic than those of the unimaginative and parochial-minded Governor. Furthermore, they had had little success in their efforts to educate Cleveland, who had kept Tilden at arm's length and had pointedly avoided consultation with him. The Governor carried a chip on his shoulder in respect to Tilden, perhaps because he felt uncomfortably on the defensive or looked with disfavor on Tilden's record as a manipulator in financial matters. Cleveland saw more of Manning, but he was aware that Manning's first loyalty was to Tilden, and Manning himself early recognized that the Governor would not be subservient to him.

A more basic reason still, until after the election of 1883, for the lack of political rapport with the Tilden-Manning partners was Cleveland's general lack of political professionalism. Cleveland acted on impulse; he took, in effect, a gambler's approach, which might lead either to fame or to failure. Tilden and Manning were coolheaded calculators. Their scientific strategy might end in defeat but never in ruin. After the defeat in 1883, however, there were definite indications that Cleveland recognized the need for political advice and political self-discipline. He was increasingly attentive to Manning, and he was politic in his handling of the Tenure of Office bill and the charges against Sheriff Davidson.

At some point, Manning decided it was expedient to use his influence to advance Cleveland. Tilden, apparently persuaded by Manning and given a promise by the Governor that he would be consulted on patronage matters, complied enough to make it possible to put the machinery into motion. Tilden announced publicly, on June 10, 1884, that "I ought not to assume a task which I have not the physical strength to carry through," thus publicly freeing Manning and other Bourbons to boom Cleveland.

In a negative way the Republicans at their national convention, held in early June, contributed greatly to the political attractiveness of Cleveland. By nominating James G. Blaine for the Presidency, they caused many Republicans to turn away toward the Democratic party, especially toward honest Grover Cleveland. These Independents, who had come to be called "Mugwumps," regarded Blaine as a dishonest timeserver. Democratic politicians were impressed by the aggressive Mugwump clamor in such important cities as Boston and New York. Notable "good government" crusaders were angry and active — such men as Carl Schurz, Henry Ward Beecher, Benjamin H. Bristow, Leverett Saltonstall, James Freeman Clarke, Richard H. Dana, Josiah Quincy, Lawrence Godkin and George W. Curtis. The Mugwumps might hold the balance of power in New York State, and their leaders were offering to work for Cleveland if he became the Democratic nominee.

Cleveland seemed to fulfill the political requirements of the era in general and of 1884 in particular. He was Governor of the largest and most politically doubtful state in the Union. He had a reputation for forthrightness and courage. His reform attacks against Tammany Hall had given him a reputation which seemed all the purer by contrast with Blaine's tarnished record. Possible Democratic candidates like Thomas F. Bayard of Delaware and Allen G. Thurman of Ohio possessed no notable political strength. Their well-known views on controversial national matters were a handicap, whereas Cleveland's own views were largely a mystery. Yet the conservatives assumed that he was safe, because he had the blessing of Bourbon potentates Tilden and Manning.

The state party convention met on June 18 at Saratoga. There Manning successfully engineered a compromise which conceded to Tammany a substantial number of delegates to the national convention and at the same time retained for the Bourbons the unit vote rule. This meant that after polling the entire state delegation all the votes would go to the candidate with majority support. Manning counted on being able to muster that majority and hence present a solid front for Cleveland.

It was not easy to accomplish, however, because, in addition to the Tammanyites, there were several other delegates with a notable lack of enthusiasm for Cleveland. The Rochester friends of William Purcell, toward whom Cleveland had shown enmity, and a few delegates bent upon obtaining the presidential nomination for Roswell P. Flower were in that camp. The outcome therefore remained in doubt until the day before the national convention opened on July 8. Then the Manning group did finally obtain the necessary majority. A thirty-seven to thirty-five vote gave Cleveland a solid front of seventy-two New York State votes. The closeness of the result showed how difficult had been Manning's task of restoring unity, after the bull-in-the-china-shop activities of the Governor.

Manning also left no stone unturned in seeking the support of delegates from other states. He showed particular interest in the national network of railroads and in the bankers and merchants along the various lines. To a startling degree he and Tilden had long since made the railroad-banker-merchant network into a Bourbon Democrat network. He could count on aid from such key figures as James J. Hill of Minnesota and Alexander Mitchell of Wisconsin. The New Yorker also sought and obtained support in the agrarian state of Missouri. Through Congressman-banker Alexander M. Dockery of Missouri Manning arranged for himself and Joseph Pulitzer a conference with John O'Day, attorney for the St. Louis and San Francisco Railway Company. The friendly meeting that ensued resulted in patronage promises. Much later, after the national convention and election were over, O'Day not only asked Manning to let him "know to whom these applications or petitions for positions should be forwarded," but he also said: "In future contests we will be able to give you as much, if not more, aid than we did at Chicago." O'Day proudly informed Manning that "the road of this corporation runs through the States of Missouri, Arkansas, Kansas, the Indian Territory, Arizona and New Mexico to Mojave, in California, and we soon expect to reach the Pacific Ocean. Our friends and delegates on the line of our road in Arkansas also stood by you."

The national convention opened in Chicago on July 8. Cleveland's strength in the convention as a whole was much greater than in his own state delegation. Upon their arrival in Chicago the Tammany delegates, conspicuous among whom were Honest John Kelly, Tom Grady and Bourke Cockran, proceeded to level a slashing attack against Cleveland. In the bars, hotel lobbies and on the floor of the convention hall itself, they did all in their power to discredit Cleveland. They falsely whispered that he was a drunkard and an anti-Catholic; they proclaimed that he was antilabor; they asserted that he could not possibly carry the vote of crucial New York State; and they insisted that the nomination should go to that champion of the people, Benjamin F. Butler. All this simply enhanced Cleveland's popularity among other delegates and the voters back home. Over much of the land Tammany had come to symbolize class impudence toward substantial people who were supposed to guide the nation's destiny; it was an embarrassing and revolting blemish on our political structure; it had fallen into the hands of selfish and disloyal charlatans who showed no hesitancy to bring about the defeat of the Democratic party if this served the personal purposes of Tammany chieftains. These were dramatic moments; they produced useful material with which to educate the home folks on the greatness of Cleveland and to accent the solid support of the "good men" in the party.

The first day, Tammany Hall delegates and the spokesmen of various alternative candidates united in a stop-Cleveland attempt. They sought to have the convention abolish the unit rule and thereby release the anti-Cleveland New York delegates from their Manning-imposed straight jacket. During the course of the debate Tammany orator Cockran reminded the convention that Cleveland did not have the unanimous support of New York State and hence should not receive the entire seventy-two delegate votes. Cleveland was "one of the men who in two years had reduced the 200,000 Democratic majority in New York to 17,000." Cockran argued in vain, and the unit rule was retained by a vote of 463 to 322. It was a highly significant victory, for those 463 votes represented a united front made up of basically discordant groups held together by the shared conviction that the party's greatest hope for victory lay in appearing to be against Tammany. Otherwise, they recognized, the Mugwump vote would not gravitate toward the Democracy.

Highlighting the convention was a heated exchange on the convention floor between two professional politicians, General Edward S. Bragg of Wisconsin and Grady of Tammany Hall. Bragg, a hardheaded, practical politician who scorned civil service reform, was dedicated to party loyalty and had recently joined the Bourbon network. The explosive Grady also disliked civil service reform, but he was more loyal to Tammany than to the national Democratic organization and to workingmen more than to Bourbons. In the course of a speech seconding the nomination of Cleveland, Bragg said that the young men of his state loved and respected Cleveland, "not only for himself, for his character, for his integrity and judgment and iron will, but they love him most for the enemies that he has made." This sally was obviously aimed at the Tammany delegates. Later in his speech he lashed out at those delegates who pretended to speak for labor and at the same time claimed that other Democrats were anti-labor. "Labor is not represented in political conventions by the soft hand of the political trickster, no matter who. The men who follow conventions and talk about the rights of labor are the Swiss contingent who place their camps wherever the prospect of profit is greatest, while honest, intelligent, horny-handed labor will be found following the old Democratic flag, thanking God that its self-styled leaders have gone where they belonged." Pointedly, Bragg attacked the delegates, and of course he meant the Tammany delegates, who talked of the rights of labor. Their own labor, he said, "has been upon the crank of the machine" — the political machine; "their study has been political chicane in the midnight conclave."

This was too much for the angry Grady. From his seat, a few feet in front of Bragg, he shouted: "On behalf of his enemies, I reciprocate that sentiment." Then a leather-lunged visitor in the gallery shouted: "A little more grape, Captain Bragg." The resourceful Civil War veteran, generously overlooking the demotion from general to captain, rose to the occasion. He leveled a pointed finger at the Tammany delegation, and exploded: "Riddleberger of Virginia, whose treachery caused a Democratic defeat in that State, would not be permitted to speak here. Gentlemen, behold the Riddlebergers of New York!" This exchange pleased loyal Democrats and also the Tammany-hating Mugwumps.

Delegates assigned to platform construction likewise performed with political wisdom, and the convention hastily ratified their handiwork. The Democrats wanted no fight among themselves, or with their Republican cousins, on matters of public policy. On the only two questions wherein conceivably there might have been a disparity in emphasis, or degree, between the Bourbon Democrats and the Republican leaders there turned out to be no discernible difference. Both parties declared for civil service reform, without presenting a positive program; both parties demanded tariff changes that would help everybody and harm nobody. As editor George William Curtis wrote: "The platforms of the two parties are practically the same."

All that remained was for Manning and fellow Bourbons formally to nominate Cleveland. On the first ballot, taken after midnight on the fourth day of convention deliberations, the count was Cleveland, 392; Bayard, 170; Thurman, 88; and Randall, 78. Manning then moved to congeal more of the Bourbons. He had a friendly visit with Pennsylvania's Samuel J. Randall, candidate of ardent high-tariff advocates and custodian of the thirty-seven votes of his own state. Upon being promised control of Pennsylvania patronage, Randall decided that Manning's choice for the nomination was satisfactory.

Nothing more was needed to bring the proceedings to a quick end. When, during the roll call on the second ballot, Pennsylvania was reached and its delegation announced for Cleveland, a stampede toward the band wagon began. State after state changed its vote, and the outcome was victory for Cleveland by a large majority. The official count was Cleveland, 682; Bayard, 81½; and Hendricks, 45½. The delegates then unanimously nominated Indiana's Thomas A. Hendricks for the Vice-Presidency.

While the weary delegates were bringing their four days of enthusiasm to a close, Cleveland was engaged in routine work at his desk in Albany. An associate, upon hearing a cannon shot, jumped up and exclaimed: "They are firing a salute, Governor, over your nomination." His secretary, Lamont, agreed. "Do you think so?" Cleveland murmured, and then slyly added: "Well, anyhow we'll finish up this work." The work was resumed, but two minutes later a telephone message confirmed the message from the cannon. Thereupon Cleveland managed to say: "By Jove, that is something, isn't it?" Indeed it was.

That evening, to a crowd of citizens who had paraded

to the mansion, the Governor delivered the first of the four speeches he made before election day. He spoke in his usual vein. With obvious sincerity, a solemn manner, ponderous phraseology and a vocabulary that reflected his legalistic and Calvinistic background, he reminded his hearers that they were soon to exercise their "power of right and sovereignty." The people were to "call in review before them their public servants and the representatives of political parties, and demand of them an account of their stewardship." The issues "to be adjudicated by the nation's great assize," he said, "are made up and are about to be submitted." To him the all-embracing issue was which party would govern more honestly and efficiently. The Democrats believe, he said, "that the people are not receiving at the hands of the party which for nearly twenty-four years has directed the affairs of the nation, the full benefits to which they are entitled, of a pure, just and economical rule; and we believe that the ascendancy of genuine Democratic principles will insure a better government, and greater happiness and prosperity to all the people."

Although he also promised that "no effort of mine shall be wanting to secure the victory," he actually played a very minor role in the campaign. Cleveland felt no inclination toward oratory, and it was very much in keeping with the views of the party managers that he remain in the background. One of his strongest assets was the fact that he had not committed himself far enough on any issue to arouse the positive enmity of any segment of the citizenry. Nobody knew, and in some cases he himself did not know, just what he might do about the tariff, monopoly, currency, land grants or veteran pensions.

Through a few brief written statements and through two public addresses he did clarify his general position on some relatively incidental items, and he reminded the public that he favored honesty, efficiency and the party platform. Although he found it difficult to contain his impulsiveness, he did defer to the judgment of his very shrewd campaign managers and advisers.

The Democratic strategy was thoroughly Bourbon in tenor. It was simply to saturate the public mind with the idea that the election of Cleveland would at last rid the government of corruption and inefficiency. This was a logical stratagem. It relieved the Democrats from disrupting party harmony by taking a definite stand on such fundamental issues as the tariff, currency and monopoly. More important, it provided the Democrats with an opportunity to hold and swell the ranks of the Mugwump contingent — that very vocal group of independent and normally Republican voters whose distaste for Blaine caused them to gravitate toward the Democratic candidate. After all, one of the reasons for Cleveland's nomination had been his acceptability by the Mugwumps.

It certainly appeared that the Democrats were a really serious challenge to the Republicans. Democratic leaders, nevertheless, were troubled in capitalizing on public interest in "good government" reform by the office-hungry party workers' distaste for the Mugwumps' widely advertised pet scheme of civil service reform. Cleveland bowed to political reality by attempting to reassure both the politicians and the reformers. He let it be known that he felt that a civil servant should not be dismissed simply because of his party affiliations, but that on the other hand he should be removed if he used his office for partisan purposes. Both the politicians and the reformers could thus hope for a better day. Party workers could dream of appointments, as a host of Republican postmasters lost their jobs because of their partisan activity; reformers could envisage the beginning of the end for the crass spoils system.

With a concrete program banned as a basis for the campaign, public interest concentrated on the personal qualities of the candidates. The Democratic strategists who planned a campaign of personalities ran the risk of a possible boomerang. They could expect that angry partisans of Blaine would spare no effort to discredit Cleveland and that the press and public would grasp at any bit of information, rumor or speculation about the candidate. The very fact that he was scarcely known aroused widespread curiosity about the burly bachelor. The citizens wished to know what he was really like, what he thought, what he knew, what he had done and what he might be apt to do. Inevitably Cleveland would be subject to extravagant attacks along with extravagant praise.

The Republicans, by nominating Blaine, helped set the stage for a campaign of character assassination. Blaine was a charming actor, both on and off the stage, but he carelessly allowed certain questionable qualities of his personal life to reach the attention of rival politicians and the public. Since 1876 it had been common knowledge that for personal financial gain he had used his political position to befriend railroad companies. When Speaker of the House of Representatives, Blaine had blocked a bill to prevent Arkansas from making a land grant to the Little Rock and Fort Smith Railroad. There had been no previous arrangement with the company, but Blaine subsequently capitalized upon his friendly act by obtaining a generous commission for selling the railroad bonds to friends in Maine. Blaine did not hesitate to employ barefaced lies to escape public condemnation for his part in the land-grant affair. Many citizens were aware that he and his large family lived comfortably in the several homes he maintained, and they wondered how he managed so well on his rather modest salary.

The exposure in 1876 of Blaine's unethical relations with the Little Rock and Fort Smith Railroad cost him the Republican presidential nomination that year, but by 1884 enough convention delegates decided it was safe to place him at the head of the ticket. This action, however, was an open invitation to the Democrats to concentrate a heavy barrage of arrows at Plumed Knight Blaine, in an effort to jog the voters' memories back to 1876, and at the same time to capitalize on the mounting public indignation against bad men in government.

The Democrats and the Mugwumps initiated the campaign of personal attack. Not only did they seize every opportunity to remind the voters of Blaine's railroad connections and his lies about the matter, but they dug up and published in September some additional evidence. Especially damaging to Blaine, who had asserted that "my whole connection with the road has been open as the day," was the publication of a letter that revealed Blaine's scheming efforts to escape condemnation and included the phrase "Burn this letter."

The Republicans, frustrated because they were forced onto the defensive, retaliated by turning a glaring light of exposure on the Democrats' symbol of integrity —

Grover Cleveland. They found an effective way to capitalize on the fact that Cleveland's consistent puritanism as a lawyer and public servant was not equaled in his personal life. Fortunately for the Republicans, the already widely circulated stories about Cleveland's saloon associations in Buffalo days prepared the public to accept what was to follow.

The Republican diversionary assault on Cleveland's past personal conduct began on July 21, when a Buffalo newspaper printed "A Terrible Tale." The tale told about Cleveland's relations in Buffalo days with the comely widow Halpin. It charged that not only was Cleveland the father of her illegitimate son but that he had crassly encouraged her to believe that he wanted to marry her and had then committed the unfortunate offspring to an orphan asylum. This account, steeped in sentiment and righteousness, was elaborated upon in like vein in subsequent articles in Republican papers throughout the nation. Another vehicle of publicity for the scandal, as well as for the one attached to Blaine, was organized religion — for the Ninth and Tenth Commandments were involved. Some religious leaders defended Cleveland and Blaine against the extreme charges, some indulged in unrestrained diatribes, but most adopted a "plague-on-both-your-houses" approach and expressed concern over the "campaign of infamy." All scandalmongers had a glorious field day — giving especial attention to Cleveland, whose relationships with the widow Halpin were more interesting than Blaine's with railroads.

The Democratic hierarchy employed the best possible approach to the crisis, a combined product of candidate Cleveland's compulsion for forthright honesty and his campaign manager's professional skill. When, upon the publication of the "Terrible Tale" a Buffalo friend telegraphed to Cleveland for instructions, the Governor wired back: "Whatever you do, tell the truth." Cleveland also prepared a detailed account of his relationship with Mrs. Halpin. Before this confession was released, campaign manager Arthur P. Gorman arrived on the scene in answer to a frantic appeal from Manning, who was well acquainted with Cleveland's proclivity for impulsive political indiscretion. Cleveland listened to the counsel of reason. He issued no statement, but assumed and maintained a public pose of dignified silence.

Many reform-minded Mugwump leaders and church leaders, however, labored valiantly to minimize the effect of the Halpin affair. The Mugwumps were in no mood to return shamefacedly to the Republican fold and to abandon the "good government" crusade. After the initial shock they tended to adopt the sensible rationalization that putting first things first called for emphasis on a candidate's public record rather than on his personal conduct. As one of the Mugwumps stated: "We are told that Mr. Blaine has been delinquent in office but blameless in private life, while Mr. Cleveland has been a model of official integrity but culpable in his personal relations. We should therefore elect Mr. Cleveland to the public office which he is so well qualified to fill, and remand Mr. Blaine to the private station which he is admirably fitted to adorn."

Some church leaders, influential as they were few in numbers, took it upon themselves to counteract the effect of extravagant outbursts from irresponsible wearers of the cloth. Notable among the Cleveland defenders was Henry

Ward Beecher, who reversed his initial repudiation of the candidate to stand squarely behind him. Another was the famous and widely beloved Boston Unitarian minister, Dr. James Freeman Clarke.

Mugwump and ministerial supporters of Cleveland were careful to base their judgment on the actual facts of the case. The Boston Committee of One Hundred, a Mugwump group, engaged an able lawyer to investigate the charges; sixteen prominent Buffalo citizens issued a report; the Reverend Dr. Clarke conferred directly with Cleveland; and the Reverend Kinsley Twining conducted an investigation in Buffalo for the *Independent*. They learned nothing significant that reflected on Cleveland's character beyond the simple fact that Cleveland, as he himself unhesitatingly refused to deny, might have been the father of the son born to Mrs. Halpin. Cleveland doubted that he was the father, but he did accept the responsibility. After Mrs. Halpin had proved to be an unsatisfactory mother, Cleveland had initiated steps that resulted in the child's adoption by a respectable and financially secure family. The Reverend Mr. Twining summed it up with the declaration that "after the preliminary offence . . . his conduct was singularly honorable, showing no attempt to evade responsibility, and doing all that he could to meet the duties involved, of which marriage was certainly not one." Between them, Mugwumps and preachers contributed substantially to the rehabilitation of the candidate's reputation. Those voters already disposed to support Cleveland were relieved by the charitable attitude of responsible leaders and clergymen.

But many conscientious citizens continued to feel that

Cleveland was evading his responsibility by failure to take the public into his confidence. On September 1, Reverend James Freeman Clarke wrote a "Private and Confidential" letter to Cleveland, stating that there "are many thousands of Republicans who are now hesitating as to their course because they do not know how to credit these accusations." He urged Cleveland to state publicly "how far you have done wrong in this matter." Clarke said that "there is something in a manly confession which clears the air, and gives assurance that he who has the courage thus to confess his sin, has already repented of it and risen above it. Politicians and men of the world would perhaps not advise you to do this, and yet it might prove in the end not only the noblest but the wisest course." The worried clergyman sent with this plea a letter written by a New Hampshire supporter of Cleveland which stated: "If Mr. Cleveland was sincere in his reply to his friends to 'tell the truth' (and we have no reason to question it), why should he now hesitate to tell it himself, tell it in his own words, tell it just as it is, unvarnished, without evasion or deception of any kind. . . . I wish he would tell it himself, over his own signature, so that every one might see and read it. However humilating it might be it would not now harm a hair of his head." Instead, it would "elevate and ennoble his character through all time, and relieve his friends from an unpleasant and trying dilemma." But Cleveland remained silent, in accordance with the advice of professional politicians.

The scandal might well have proved disastrous. But luckily its exposure came very early in the campaign, allowing the public's shock to subside while publication of factual accounts and reasoned opinions reduced the scandal to smaller proportion in the public mind.

The depiction of Blaine as an unrestrained public plunderer and Cleveland as a town drunk and debaucher was just a part of the material used to fill the vacuum of a campaign devoid of issues. Hence, lingering Civil War prejudices, pension-conscious war veterans, the Catholic issue, anti-British sentiment, nativism and prohibition received much attention.

As the outlandish, issue-starved campaign approached its end, it was apparent to both sides that the outcome was very much in doubt. The election hinged on the results in the four doubtful states, Connecticut, Indiana, New Jersey and New York. Democrats took satisfaction in the fact that there were many Mugwumps in those states and that in Indiana the popular Hendricks was their Vice-Presidential candidate. They were more than a little nervous, however, about the situation in New York State.

The closeness of the New York contest and the paucity of real issues exaggerated the importance of a variety of elusively vague factors, each of which threatened to upset the normal pattern of voting in the state. There was, for example, wonder over the effect of Roscoe Conkling's pronounced hatred for fellow Republican Blaine, the prohibitionist element, the Catholics, the effects of the 1884 depression, the size of the Mugwump group, the strength of the third-party tickets, Tammany Hall, upstate city machines, and many situations involving local resentments, hassles and jockeying.

The Democrats pinned much of their hope for carrying crucial New York on the Mugwump and the Prohibition party vote. Although most of the latter would not go to Cleveland, but rather to Prohibition candidate John P. St. John, it would come from the normally Republican ranks. This loss to the Republicans, nevertheless, might well prove too little to overcome the unpopularity of Cleveland among New York workingmen. His demonstrated indifference to the demands of wage earners in general and his hostility to labor unions in particular caused concern. Even in Cleveland's own Buffalo, labor organizations entered politics to defeat him for the Presidency. Labor editor Swinton, in his *John Swinton's Paper,* wrote in July that Cleveland "watched like a lynx for every bill in the interests of the working classes that he might put his foot upon it."

Some of the labor vote, partly because of the widespread unemployment and fear of further unemployment, would go to the National Greenback party ticket, headed by colorful Ben Butler. In fact, Republican managers quietly subsidized Butler's canvass, thus frustrating subsequent Democratic efforts to persuade Butler to withdraw. Blaine was expected to garner a substantially larger vote from the workingmen than was customary for Republican candidates. This would be despite, and not because of, Blaine's and the Republicans' general labor record. It would also be despite a particular situation in New York City, where the printers' union, with a membership of 3,500, launched an anti-Blaine campaign to punish the Republican party for its refusal to repudiate the New York *Tribune* as a party organ. The *Tribune* and the union were engaged in a wage-scale battle.

The Republicans' increased labor vote might come through a side door. Blaine might ensnare the workingmen on their way to Catholic Mass, rather than on their way home from twelve hours of laborious work in sweat-shops at near-starvation wages. Blaine was popular among the Catholics — especially the Irish Catholics, who normally voted Democratic and whose voting strength was about a half million in the nation, over a quarter of which was in New York State. He had warmed the cockles of many an Irish-American heart by twisting the British Lion's tail; his mother had been an Irish Catholic and a sister was Mother Superior of a Catholic convent. Too, it was widely circulated, although with complete unfairness, that Cleveland was a "Presbyterian bigot" and a "cowardly bigot." The more-than-severe anti-Cleveland attacks that Irishmen John Kelly, Tom Grady and other Tammany leaders had perpetrated during the previous two years had helped prepare the political soil for Republican cultivation.

Tammany's lack of enthusiasm for Cleveland was a major handicap in New York State, even though it was an advantage in other states. Chieftain Kelly retreated, for reasons of political expediency, from his initial open hostility to Cleveland and forced himself and most of his subordinates into an endorsement of the Cleveland-Hendricks ticket, but much damage had been done already.

As the campaign went into its final week, the eyes of the nation focused ever more sharply on New York. While the betting showed Cleveland slightly favored in the other doubtful states, it showed Blaine slightly the favorite in New York. But Cleveland had to capture that state to win.

Then, suddenly, two events on Wednesday, October 29 — seven days before the election — altered the outlook. On that day the very weary, and hence unwary, Blaine began a round of political activity in New York City. In the morning he met with a group of clergymen, whose spokesman, the Reverend Samuel D. Burchard, informed Blaine that the antecedents of the Democratic party were "Rum, Romanism, and Rebellion." Misfortune and carelessness on the Republican side, compared with attentiveness and speedy action on the Democratic side, resulted very shortly in "Rum, Romanism, and Rebellion" handbills, posters and headlines in every city with large Catholic populations. By that time it was too late for the Republicans effectively to counteract the full force of the hurricane. It blew hitherto undecided Catholic voters off the fence and into the Democratic shelters. Many Catholics now recalled the reputation of the Republicans as a party permeated with Burchards — self-righteous and overbearing nativists. They also recalled the Republican record on puritanical liquor legislation and parochial schools. How many votes the Democrats thereby acquired remained a moot question. But without their acquisition Cleveland would have lost the election.

The other unfortunate experience for the Republican ticket on that disastrous October 29 was Blaine's presence at a "prosperity dinner" at Delmonico's. Two hundred of the nation's wealthiest men gathered there to honor the Republican candidate. The sponsors, headed by Cyrus W. Field, were motivated in part by the opportunity the dinner afforded to obtain campaign funds. Republican campaign manager Stephen B. Elkins was astute enough to oppose the step, but his efforts were not enough to halt the moguls accustomed to ruling. They assumed that the lesser persons wanted it that way, for humble people had confidence in the superior judgment of men of great accomplishments. On this particular occasion the banquet managers decided not to display everything that went on, so they excluded all newspaper reporters after the banqueters had feasted and then retired to the parlors. An Associated Press reporter, but no others, was nevertheless permitted to observe the banquet itself, to see that present, among the two hundred, were Jay Gould, Russell Sage, Andrew Carnegie, Levi P. Morton, Charles Tiffany and William M. Evarts. The reporter heard Blaine deliver an address that ran the gamut of superlatives in praise of plutocracy. Next day's newspapers carried many scathing editorial comments on the affair. The New York *World* presented its readers with an unusually large front-page cartoon, captioned "The Royal Feast of Belshazzar Blaine and the Money Kings." Therein Blaine and the moguls were depicted at a table laden with terrapin, canvasback duck and champagne, with the added feature of a hungry family begging for crumbs. October 29, as the New York *World* reported, was "Mr. Blaine's black Wednesday."

It was even blacker than it appeared on the surface, for manager Elkins later revealed that at Delmonico's the campaign contributions were "much less generous than had been expected." Most wealthy men were willing to have Blaine in the White House, and certainly they did not want to antagonize him as long as there was a possibility that he would be there. But they set a limit to the amount of money they deemed necessary to demonstrate their friendly attitude. Some millionaires even decided that part of their campaign budget should go to the Democrats, where friendship was also important and from whom there was nothing to fear.

Finally Tuesday, November 4, arrived, bringing rain and an end to the crazy campaign. Cleveland captured, although very narrowly, all the doubtful states and thereby narrowly won the election. He carried New York by a plurality of 1,149 votes out of the 1,167,000 total, and in the nation as a whole his plurality was about 25,000 more than opponent Blaine's.

It was a victory for practical politics. There had been as much political shrewdness in the Democratic camp as mismanagement in the Republican camp. A generation of unbroken victories in presidential elections had made Republican leaders careless, cocksure and smug. They were unaware of changes in the prejudices and convictions, the fears and aspirations, the economic and social status of the men who cast the votes. The Democrats, on the other hand, had been fighting their way upward by looking for every dent and hole in the Republican armor. Bourbonism and Tammanyism had narrowed Democratic opportunities. But the Mugwump movement gave the party its opportunity. Mugwump support, added to the practiced Democratic skill in building and managing city machines and sniping at Republican corruption, plutocracy and nativism, turned the trick.

While the outcome was a victory for practical politics, it was also to a degree a triumph for the cause of good government. The very fact that optimistic, wishful-thinking reformers claimed it to be such and that tongue-in-cheek professional politicians expediently agreed went far to advance the demand for an era of reform. If they expected to remain popular, the Democrats now had to deliver results or justify their failure. That Blaine was denied the Presidency was something of a victory for the cause, because his victory would have been conspicuous evidence of public indifference to integrity in high places. His substantial vote indicated that there was indifference aplenty, but his defeat stamped him and the cause he represented as a failure. Whether or not Cleveland would implement this psychological impetus for good government remained to be seen.

This was a victory for practical politics and for the cause of "good government," but it was even more a victory for big business and a defeat for workingmen and farmers. The voters had been cast in their customary role of voting for rule by business simply because they were offered no alternative. Cleveland was manifestly a man of honesty, but a man with the conviction that to serve business was to serve the nation as a whole.

V

Businessmen's President

As CLEVELAND'S thoughts focused on the role
that lay before him, he emphasized implementation of
the narrowly limited Bourbon-Mugwump program. He
would strive for more honest and efficient administration;
he would staff the public offices with efficient and trust-
worthy people, recruited from the Democratic party; and
he would be especially friendly toward business leaders,
who were doing so much to add to the wealth and well-
being of the nation. This program, demanded by the most
articulate and most powerful groups in the land, harmo-
nized with Cleveland's own temperament, knowledge and
experience.

Cleveland approached the Presidency as though he were
a martyr, who would doggedly perform the unpleasant
chores of government. Shortly after the election he said
to his close friend and former law partner, Bissell, that
he looked upon the "four years next to come as a dread-
ful self-inflicted penance for the good of my country. I
can see no pleasure in it and no satisfaction, only a hope
that I may be of service to my people." When worried

or angry, Cleveland donned a hair shirt and squirmed in it self-righteously. That was his mood during the weeks following the election. The knowledge that during the campaign it was reported over the whole land that he was a "moral leper" had embarrassed and angered him and left him anything but joyful as he approached the nation's highest office. Once elected, he found himself pathetically lonely. Jockeying for position, even by friends, left him stranded in a crowd of associates whose hands seemed to be outstretched.

Cleveland conscientiously and carefully selected his Cabinet. His approach to the task reflected his political views and those of the dominant forces in the Democratic party. In the end his Cabinet represented the fusion of interests that were to control the Democratic party and were greatly to influence the nation during the "Cleveland era."

The individual members of the Cabinet were men of strength of will — intelligent, conservative, self-assured, endowed with a sense of responsibility and with records of success in politics, law or business. They might well have been Republican chieftains — whom they very much resembled. Actually they were members of a closely related clan, the Bourbon Democracy: men with closer affinity with railroads than with factories; with leanings toward lower tariff rates; distrustful of extensive governmental regulation, subsidies and paternalism.

The Cabinet membership was impressive in the extent to which it symbolized the national scope of the Bourbon empire. Each major region was represented — the East, the South and the West. Yet the Cabinet was not truly representative, for three important groups had no spokesmen within it. Nowhere among its members was there a champion of the farmers, who constituted overwhelmingly the largest segment of the population; or of the rapidly growing wage-earner class; or of the Southern Negroes.

Easterners filled three Cabinet posts. The two New York appointees symbolized the blending in the national Bourbon leadership of the 1868–1884 Tilden-Manning dominance and the Cleveland-Whitney 1884–1896 combination. Manning, Secretary of the Treasury, was appointed because of a precampaign promise to Tilden, who had made the appointment a condition for his endorsement of the Cleveland candidacy. Whitney on the other hand was unreservedly attached to Cleveland. The ties between them had grown ever stronger from the 1882 election onward. Cleveland admired the forty-three-year-old Whitney as a lawyer, financier and public officer. This scion of an old New England family had demonstrated superior ability as Corporation Counsel of New York from 1875 to 1882 and thereafter as a key promoter in the consolidation of the New York street railway system. In this highly profitable manipulation he worked in close alliance with shrewd and dynamic Thomas Fortune Ryan and with the wealthy Widener group of Philadelphia. The traction syndicate in which Whitney was so actively engaged was finally to emerge, in 1886, as perhaps the first holding company in the nation. This device was developed for the syndicate by Cleveland's political friend and law associate, Francis Lynde Stetson.

Whitney, meanwhile, spent much effort to bring about the nomination and election of Cleveland. During the campaign he personally gave $20,000, a sum which ranked him third or fourth among the contributors, and very effectively sought assistance from others. Whitney enjoyed behind-the-scene politics more than actual office-holding. But he could not bring himself to refuse a Cabinet post as Secretary of the Navy.

William C. Endicott of Massachusetts was chosen Secretary of War, in a shrewdly devised scheme to be friendly toward the Mugwumps without actually placing one of them in the Cabinet. He spoke their language on matters of "good government" reform. An old-time conservative Whig who had joined the Democracy in 1856, Endicott found it easy to get along well with business-minded Republicans of the post-War era. A Republican Governor had even appointed this wealthy, aristocratic, well-read, and widely traveled Salem lawyer to the state Supreme Court bench.

Cleveland's selection of Cabinet members representing the South and the West was more difficult, the new President being woefully unacquainted with those regions and their leaders. The task demanded special care because these appointments would reveal his attitude and intentions toward the Democratic organizations in these perennially restless and sometimes insurgent agrarian regions. He might indicate a willingness to make concessions, to compromise, to ignore the unrest or to make perfectly clear that he would not tolerate any deviation from complete Bourbonism. He chose the latter course and thereby forestalled the emergence within the party of a West-South agrarian alliance that might threaten Eastern industrial control of the nation.

Cleveland's uncompromising insistence on recognizing only pure Bourbons in both regions was a double insurance against agrarianism. The continued adherence of either region to the Eastern high command would be enough to avoid catastrophe. With the South alone still loyal, it was possible to win the Presidency through an East-South combination. With the West alone still loyal, the Democracy there would at least be kept from becoming a popular vehicle for agrarian radicalism.

Cleveland invited two important conservative Southern leaders into his Cabinet — Lucius Q. C. Lamar, from Mississippi, as Secretary of the Interior, and Augustus H. Garland, from Arkansas, as Attorney General. Both led in the post-Civil War effort to restore their regions to Southern white political-social domination and to project the industrial revolution southward. These men scorned the Thomas Jefferson-Andrew Johnson cult, which wanted the South to be a land of small farms and shops, owned by their operators; they likewise scorned the dreamers who with nostalgia wished to restore the South to the "sweet magnolia," plantation way of life. They were neither agrarian radicals nor old Southern Bourbons. They belonged to a group that encouraged industrial advance and unblinkingly accepted white supremacy.

Long-bearded Lamar, gentle and talkative, well read in law and philosophically minded, appeared to be an easygoing town father whose lovable characteristics had kept him from retirement to oblivion. Actually, however, he was very much an inner participant in post-War public affairs. Before the War he was a conservative Democrat, who drafted Mississippi's secession ordinance, served two years in the Confederate Army and thereafter was one of the South's Redeemers. He was one of the principals in effecting the Compromise of 1877, which gave

Hayes the Presidency and the South promises of Northern Republican aid for railroads, internal improvements and political plums. Lamar was very much interested in railroads. He found ample outlet for this enthusiasm as a corporation lawyer and as a member of the House of Representatives (1873–1877) and of the United States Senate (1877–1885). In 1877 the *Nation,* reacting to a railroad bill that Lamar introduced in the House, commented on the Mississippian's friendly cooperation with railroad promoter Tom Scott and revealed that Lamar was "representative, *par excellence,* of the South in the new order of things." Lamar was also a firm gold currency defender. While a few Redeemers bent to the silverite wind that swept the South, Lamar made no concessions, real or pretended. In 1877 he voted against the Bland silver bill, despite instructions from the Mississippi legislature to support the measure.

Tall, broad-shouldered Garland was a friendly, down-to-earth fellow, who proudly proclaimed that he had never owned a dress suit. He was an able lawyer and politician. Like most of the Redeemers, but unlike Lamar, he had been a Whig in the ante-bellum days. His Redeemer position was very evident during his governorship of Arkansas (1874–1876) and his United States senatorship (1877–1885). He equaled Lamar in unflinching support of the Republican-Redeemer arrangements that made Hayes President and later, like Lamar and the other Redeemers, found his real political home in the national Bourbon Democracy.

The West received one place on the Cabinet, that of William F. Vilas of Wisconsin as Postmaster General. Thereby Cleveland drove a potentially large spike into the coffin of the silver and antimonopoly agitators in the ranks of the Western agrarian Democracy. The 1868 East-West Bourbon alliance had not broken, but it had been threatened with destruction in the 1870's. However, the Granger uprising had been brought under control, and the currency inflation hurricane had spent its fury. By 1884 there was relative calm. Luck and hard work had saved the Bourbons, but much remained to be done to insure future security.

Vilas had managed to ride out the storm and had emerged as a simon-pure Bourbon. As a young man new to politics he had become vaguely identified with the Granger upsurge that defeated the Republicans in Wisconsin, but immediately thereafter by becoming a railroad lawyer and an outspoken defender of the gold standard he left no doubts regarding his position. During the 1878 campaign, when the inflationists were conspicuous in the Wisconsin Democracy, able Democratic campaign orator Vilas found it convenient to spend much of his time on fishing trips. He was a brilliant, well-educated, efficient, hard-working lawyer, businessman and political leader. Politically he had early attached his star to the New York Tilden-Manning group and at the same time refused to waste time seeking elective office in overwhelmingly Republican Wisconsin. At the 1884 national convention, when he was forty-three years old, Vilas successfully served as chairman. Later he made a favorable impression on Cleveland when chairman of the committee to notify the Governor of his nomination. After the election Cleveland talked with Vilas and conferred with others about him. A conversation between Iowa state Democratic chairman Moses M. Ham and Cleveland revealed something about both Vilas and Cleveland. In reply to the question regarding Vilas's reputation in the West, Ham emphasized Vilas's oratory and his popularity "everywhere and particularly with the best element of the democratic party." In reply to Cleveland's question on Vilas's professional standing, Ham reported that Vilas was in sole charge of the North Western Railroad's interests in the state. He added that of course "there is a small granger element still existing in the west which always opposes an officer of a corporation for any position, but it has little weight or influence now, it is not much considered in our politics and ought not to be." Cleveland, it was reported, thereupon said: "That is simply a matter of business. It is the duty of an attorney to seek the best clients and remain faithful to them, and to use all honorable means to enhance his emoluments and increase his experience and his fame in the profession to which he devotes the best years of his life." Cleveland added that "great corporations always secure if possible the best legal talent to protect their interests and in this they show much shrewdness and it is also economy."

The other Cabinet officer, Thomas F. Bayard, Secretary of State, was more a representative of the respectable Democratic party tradition than of a particular region or of a dynamic economic-political force. There was much more meaning in the fact that he was one of a long line of Bayards who had served with dignified distinction in high public offices than in the fact that he came from Delaware. Bayard had been a United States Senator for sixteen years and had demonstrated a conservatism and caution pleasing to the purest Bourbons. He was somewhat detached from the workaday world of business pressure groups, political rewards, compromises, deals, scrambles and personal temperamental displays of stubbornness, dogmatism, fear, sentimentality, ambition and greed. Uncompromisingly dedicated to free trade, sound money and limited government precepts, Bayard was a true doctrinaire Democrat. He was well equipped to conduct American foreign affairs in the manner Cleveland preferred — with dignity and firmness, and totally without imperialistic aims or jingoistic postures.

Nothing about Cleveland's Cabinet appointments stirred the excitement of the public or the press. The President had done about as expected. The same was true of his inaugural address, although there was drama to the occasion. The hosts of Democrats who descended upon Washington were jubilant, and the unprecedented manner in which Cleveland delivered his inaugural address was truly impressive. He spoke without a manuscript, relying on his remarkable gift for almost instantaneous memorization. The content of the message, however, was far from arresting. The keynote in the brief address, although clear, was too familiar and too flat in tone. "The people demand reform in the administration of the government, and the application of business principles to public affairs."

As Cleveland began the actual work of being President, it was perfectly evident that he would try to keep the clear tone of his inaugural keynote bright and fresh. He launched upon the task as though he were a man possessed. Giving little or no thought to legislation, Cleveland spent the whole time at his first Cabinet meeting and most of the time during the next six meetings discussing departmental reform.

His Cabinet members approached their tasks with zeal. They obviously wanted to demonstrate to Cleveland and to the public that they were equal to their assignments. They were self-conscious, knowing that more people than normal were watching the administration. The public was curious about how the inexperienced Democratic leaders would conduct affairs now that their party had obtained actual power after twenty-four years. Cleveland's utterances had focused public attention so much more on the administrative than on the legislative branch that the administrators, knowing they were being watched carefully, were inspired and felt obligated to apply more than their normal effort. They also had more than usual opportunity. It was very helpful to have a President who used his power and influence to help his subordinates fight off the special-interest pressure groups and the unwanted jobseeker element that always threatened honest, efficient and economical administration. Because their party had been out of power for so long they could start with a clean broom and find plenty of use for it. Inevitably the long regime of the opposition party had resulted in an accumulation of habitual carelessness and inefficiency, entrenched favoritism, and jobholders without useful jobs to perform or without ability to handle any jobs.

Cleveland and those Cabinet members from the North performed like men working against time. Those from the South, most notably Lamar, were more philosophical about it all, but even they, caught in the stream of action and with some aggressive subordinates, had dynamic departments. Contrary to the predictions of many, Cleveland and his Cabinet proved that the Democratic party could administer. There were no startling disclosures of scandals like the Crédit Mobilier or the Whisky Ring of the Grant era, but many lesser instances of corruption were uncovered. There were no sweeping new policies or programs, but the departments were efficiently administered.

Cleveland and his Cabinet officers demonstrated that the Democratic party had at least as much ability to conduct affairs as the Republicans. They performed, with rare exceptions, as Bourbons, but with no expectation of increasing their personal bank balances. In private most of the Cabinet were intimately connected with railroad corporations, but in their public affairs they did not hesitate to oppose railroads whenever the corporations interfered with the honest and efficient performance of the federal departments. This did not mean that they or Cleveland were among the crusaders bent upon forcing a radical reorganization of the Union Pacific in order to collect the millions of dollars which that road had borrowed from the government and which it showed no willingness or ability to pay. Nor did it mean they went out of their way to push forward the demand for railroad regulation that in 1887 culminated in passage of the Interstate Commerce Act. But within their own individual bailiwicks they were out to make good records. Hence, while the railroads received the friendly treatment that was a natural expression of Bourbonism, the railroads were in turn expected to cooperate in the endeavor for more honesty and efficiency in the government.

The extent to which one member placed his desire to do well in his job above his Bourbonism, when the two interests happened to clash, was clearly manifested in Secretary Vilas's conduct as Postmaster General. This able and hard-working administrator became incensed at certain railroads for their laxity and for overcharges in hauling mail. The roads refused to accept reasonable compensation, to meet reasonable standards of efficiency, and to provide reasonable conditions of safety for mail clerks. Vilas made every effort to reach satisfactory agreements with the railroads. When he failed, he urged Congress, fruitlessly, to provide the means for government ownership and operation of mail cars.

Vilas confronted an administrative problem that seemingly defied solution through normal means. In this instance private enterprise meant a constant and impossible contest between the seekers of profits and the seekers of efficient and economical public service. He moved therefore all the way to the logical alternative, a system of unhampered operation. In this Vilas acted, as was also typical of Cleveland, without apparent thought for the broader implications of his solution. He did not reflect that if it were better to have government ownership and operation of mail cars it might also be better to have government ownership of the locomotives that hauled the cars. His grievance did not lead him that far. He did discover that government-owned mail cars could save the department at least a million and a half dollars annually and that the cost of building the cars would be less than the amount the government paid out in car rentals in one year alone. The government could also, he argued, promise better and safer service. The time was not ripe, however, and Vilas failed. When Congress finally acted, in 1916, during the Progressive era, the reform inaugurated was strict regulation rather than government ownership.

The most constructive departmental achievement was

Whitney's start on the building of a new navy. In 1883, during Chester A. Arthur's administration, a report of a naval advisory board showed that the navy was hopelessly outmoded. Congress thereupon authorized the rapid construction of three steel cruisers and a dispatch boat. At the close of the Arthur administration, Congress authorized four more ships. William E. Chandler, then Secretary of the Navy, proved as poor an administrator as he was a gifted politician. Chaos resulted.

Whitney, with Cleveland's close cooperation, reorganized the Navy Department and launched the building program. More important was Whitney's successful attempt to induce the domestic steel industry to expand its facilities and thereby remove the necessity for future reliance on foreign ship steel. It was an accomplishment of great importance for the future. Ironically, although the "big navy" enthusiasts of a few years later had reason to feel grateful, Cleveland was not a "big navy" man, a jingoist or an imperialist. He simply wished the United States to possess a navy sufficient to protect its position in the world.

Though the navy program was the most constructive result of Cleveland's crusade for efficiency, the work of the Interior Department was unsurpassed as an expression of Cleveland's moral indignation at graft, waste, greed and exploitation. The President wasted no time in directing Secretary Lamar to remedy the truly lamentable situation in the public domain and in the Indian territories. The amount of good Western land available, or that could be made available, for settlement, mining or logging was fast declining. This fact in itself did not distress Cleveland and his associates; in fact, they tried to facilitate speedier settlement and speedier utilization of untapped mineral and forest lands. It was the manner rather than the substance that angered Cleveland. Cattle barons, land companies, crooked surveyors, logging and lumbering concerns, unprincipled politicians and public officials, and railroad corporations employed every conceivable illegal or shady device to grab public- and Indian-owned land. Cleveland, Lamar and able Land Commissioner William A. J. Sparks launched a reform drive. They sent special agents into the West to investigate, ordered removal of fences that cattlemen had illegally constructed on the public domain, checked exploitation and robbery of Indians, carefully scrutinized land entries and removed unsatisfactory officials.

The railroad land grants posed one of the most serious problems. Until Congress put a stop to the practice in 1871, the government had been lavish in its donations to railroad corporations. There were provisions in the grants for forfeiture of land if the railroads failed to comply with certain conditions. At the time Cleveland became President the railroads retained millions of acres of land clearly long since subject to forfeiture. In addition, when it had not been possible to grant land along the proposed railroad route, the companies had been allowed to choose "indemnity lands" elsewhere. Officials friendly to the railroads had generously set aside choice areas from which the corporations could make selection whenever they wished. Not only did this indefinitely keep huge regions from legal homesteading, but it afforded the railroads an opportunity to play a cat-and-mouse game. They could wait until a homesteader had innocently settled upon and developed a quarter section of land and then elect it as an indemnity land. Cleveland, through an executive order, managed to end this practice. In this case he proved to be less narrowly legalistic than Secretary Lamar and Attorney General Garland. His order overruled a legal decision of Garland's, which Lamar felt expressed the proper position.

Early in 1887 Congress, with Cleveland's sincere endorsement, passed the historic Dawes Act which inaugurated the experiment of Americanization of the Indians. The way was opened to them to become citizens of the United States and to own land as individuals instead of as members of their tribes. Cleveland, who was genuinely shocked at the white man's exploitation of Indians and their property, believed this measure opened the way for more justice. He thought it wise, however, to apply it gradually, because it was an untested approach to the Indian problem.

Yet when some of his subordinates demonstrated more interest in general economic progress than in paternalistic sheltering of Indians, Cleveland raised no objections. Key figure in this development was Vilas, who in 1887 became Secretary of the Interior after Lamar was appointed to the Supreme Court. Vilas wasted no time in helping loggers purchase timber from the Indians on the land alloted to them in northern Wisconsin. A Congressional investigation revealed no dishonesty on Vilas's part, but did show that this dynamic Westerner on the Cabinet had true Bourbon zeal for rapid material progress. He sincerely believed that deserving Indians and the nation as a whole could not fail to benefit when natural laws of economics were allowed to operate freely, unhampered by governmental paternalism. In his opinion logging activity afforded Indians cash for their trees, job opportunities and land cleared for their crops. Cleveland agreed. He expected only that the transaction be carried on with honesty, efficiency and economy.

Attorney General Garland in one notable instance exhibited a lack of understanding of the requirements of disinterested public service. Before becoming Attorney General he owned one tenth of the stock of the Pan-Electric Company and was the lawyer for the concern. He retained the stock after joining the Cabinet. The only asset of the company was an uncertain title to the Rogers telephone patent. The Bell Company was using the invention and claimed priority to its patent. Hence the Pan-Electric stock would have value only if it could win a court case against the Bell Company. Perhaps Pan-Electric promoters were seeking aid in bringing the matter to adjudication when they offered gifts of stock to various Congressmen. In any case, in 1885, while Garland was vacationing in Arkansas, the Solicitor General initiated a suit against the Bell Company. Garland later claimed that this action was without his knowledge. Cleveland ordered the suit dropped and the matter referred to the Interior Department. Early in 1886, however, Lamar decided to continue the legal action. In November a circuit court dismissed the case on the ground of lack of jurisdiction. Meanwhile Republican newspapers gleefully, and Mugwump newspapers indignantly, attacked Garland. He remained in the Cabinet, but his indiscretion blighted his career and embarrassed the administration.

As the months unfolded, Cleveland had reason to take pride in the results of his concentration on administrative matters. His supporters were gratified that even though Republican partisans naturally sniped at and belittled some of this activity, they found little of real importance to criticize. The less partisan element seemed to be relatively indifferent to what went on.

This initial success gave Cleveland more confidence in himself, and he gradually became more relaxed. He worked hard but found time for companionship with close friends. Lamont, the private secretary he brought with him from Albany, was a joy to Cleveland. He had close and loyal friendships with some of his Cabinet members, especially with Vilas. There was an air of informal cordiality at the White House, especially when Cleveland's rather stern sister Rose was not too much in evidence. Out-of-town guests frequented the White House. Mrs. Oscar Folsom, widow of Cleveland's close friend of Buffalo days, and her daughter Frances were among the first, and they remained for a fortnight. Others, from Buffalo and Albany, came and went. Cleveland was often too busy to see much of them except at mealtime, but he liked having people close at hand.

In his relations with the public he conducted himself with the dignity that befitted his high office, but he longed to escape into the more plebian environment he loved. He was not too happy about the French chef inherited from the elegance of the Arthur tenancy. "I must go to dinner," he wrote in a letter to Bissell, "but I wish it was to eat pickled herring, Swiss cheese and a chop at Louis' instead of the French stuff I shall find." Certainly, too, he found his brief fishing experiences along the Potomac very unsatisfactory compared with the expeditions of Buffalo days.

Finally, in the summer of 1885, Cleveland broke out of

his harness and headed for the woods. After attending Grant's funeral in New York, he and some cronies betook themselves to the Adirondacks. They tramped far into the wilderness to a very crude cabin. The long, arduous march was too much for Cleveland. He was grossly overweight, and insufficient exercise in Washington had ill prepared him for such activity. After a couple of days, however, he was able to join the rest, except for deer hunting. They spent so much time fishing, hunting, playing cards and consuming food and whisky that they devoted only four or five hours out of twenty-four to sleep.

In the spring of 1886 rumors were rampant that Cleveland intended to be married. He did not deny the report, but he was impatient with reporters who sought an official confirmation of the closely guarded secret. As late as May 17 it was not known for sure whether the suspected bride was to be Miss Folsom or Mrs. Folsom. Cabinet members seemed as much in the dark as the outside world. After the death of Cleveland's friend and law partner, Oscar Folsom, in 1875, Cleveland had been asked to administer the will and thereafter took great personal interest in Mrs. Folsom and her little daughter Frances.

When Miss Folsom was a student at Wells College and Cleveland was Governor, he obtained permission from Mrs. Folsom to correspond with her attractive daughter. He wrote to Frances often, sent flowers, entertained her and Mrs. Folsom in the Governor's mansion in Albany and then in the White House. Gradually affection became romance.

He waited until after her graduation from college before proposing marriage. They became engaged in August, 1885, following an exchange of affectionate letters. Cleveland later remarked that he often said to his wife: "Poor girl, you never had any courting like other girls." But he added: "It is true I did say some things to her one night, when we were walking together in the East Room, when she was here visiting my sister."

Miss Folsom and her mother were traveling in Europe in the spring of 1886. When they arrived in New York on May 27 they were met at the boat by Lamont and escorted to the Gilsey House. They were considerably upset at the time, having learned by wire during the voyage home of the death of Miss Folsom's grandfather. Lamont left them and returned to Washington to report to Cleveland on the wedding plans. Miss Folsom had selected the following Wednesday, June 2, for the ceremony, to be conducted in the White House; she wished it to be a simple, small affair in keeping with the family's period of mourning for her grandfather. The afternoon of May 28 Cleveland told the news to his Cabinet members, and that evening he made the news public. The engagement had taken place about a year before, when Miss Folsom was twenty-two and Cleveland was forty-eight, but it had been kept secret even from Miss Folsom's closest friends.

The wedding was performed at seven o'clock in the evening, on June 2, in the Blue Room of the White House, by the Reverend Dr. Byron Sunderland, Cleveland's pastor, assisted by the Reverend William N. Cleveland, Cleveland's brother. Members of the Cabinet and their wives were present (with the exception of Garland, who declined), a few relatives and several close friends, including Bissell. The bride was unattended. Her wedding dress of corded ivory satin with its fifteen-foot train had been purchased in Europe, but, according to the New York *Times,* "it was the woman at whom the women looked rather than the dress." The bride was a tall, handsome, light brunette, with large blue eyes. She had dignity, charm and elegance. At the close of the simple Presbyterian service, during the informal reception and supper which followed in the state dining room, the President and Mrs. Cleveland slipped away for a honeymoon at Deer Park in western Maryland.

The bride had proudly shown her wedding gift from the President, a beautiful diamond necklace, but the other gifts, in deference to the wishes of Cleveland, were not on display at the reception. Some people had been concerned about the matter of suitable gifts to compliment the bride, knowing Cleveland's opposition to receiving presents of any kind, but Whitney, Vilas and Bissell all gave gifts of diamond jewelry to the bride. Endicott sent four large, elegant silver candlesticks, and Lamar a gold smelling bottle set in diamonds. One newspaper estimated that "nearly $100,000 worth of presents had reached the White House by six o'clock and more were doubtless in transit."

Garland's absence from the wedding was attributed by some to his reluctance to wear a dress suit, but it was also known that at the death of his wife, some years ago, he had made a vow never to enter into social festivities again. He had kept this vow throughout the years, not even attending his own son's wedding, and had devoted his time when not at the office to the care of his aged mother.

Everyone in the country seemed delighted with Cleveland's choice of bride, and the marriage appeared to be a real love match. A Cabinet officer's wife said: "You may depend that the President will not work himself to death now. He has begun a new life . . . you may look for a decided change in favor of leisure. . . . He has not been waiting these dozen years for her, not to try to make her happy now. He is really an unselfish man and one of the kindest." Cleveland's marriage was a very happy one. Henceforth he participated increasingly in the social life which the young Mrs. Cleveland enjoyed so much. She brought grace and life to the White House, fulfilling in every way her difficult role as First Lady.

Even though Cleveland conducted his office very much as though he were still Mayor of Buffalo or Governor of New York, he seemed unable to take the Presidency in his stride. Actually, he had not learned how to live congenially in the world of politics, nor was it something he could be taught. He lacked the broad view that stimulates public leaders to great purposes and he did not enjoy the maneuvering, compromising and diversionary tactics and the use of blandishments that are second nature to born politicians. He seemed unable to crusade successfully for anything that required him to build an effective following among the politicians and the voters.

These limitations and his excellent qualities were very apparent in his handling of the patronage. He neither enjoyed the task nor evidenced especial ability for it. Although his conscientiousness saved him from complete failure, his weaknesses limited him to a mediocre civil service record. The difficulties posed, however, were such that even a genius could not have been wholly successful.

Cleveland showed more conscientiousness than wisdom in dealing directly with the horde of office seekers. He personally examined hundreds of applications and spent many evenings with Vilas reviewing the qualifications of prospective postmasters — even fourth-class postmasters. While he doubtless had a good time with Vilas, drinking beer and poring over bundles of papers, he was obviously annoyed with the daytime crowd of eager office seekers. He was often brusque with them, habitually grumbling to friends, associates and newsmen about the patronage-seeker nuisances. Typical was the exclamation to a friend: "My God, what is there in this office that any man should ever want to get into it!"

The most difficult part of the task was to achieve a satisfactory balance among the rival claimants. Civil service reformers, most notably the Mugwumps, who had done much to secure Cleveland's election, were very vocal in their opinions on how patronage should be handled. They were especially eager to dictate policy on removal of Republican incumbents. Editors George William Curtis and Edwin Lawrence Godkin and politician-reformer Carl Schurz used their considerable abilities to keep Cleveland and the public aware of civil service reform, and the National Civil Service Reform League worked valiantly. They tried to keep alive the memories of Grantism, the assassination of Garfield by a disappointed spoilsman, the passage in 1883 of the Pendleton Act which created the Civil Service Commission and the 1884 Democratic-Mugwump campaign promises for good government. They leaned heavily on statistics and emphasized that Cleveland should bring about a party balance in the civil service, allowing both Republicans and Democrats fifty per cent of the appointive offices.

For a short time it appeared that Cleveland would go a

considerable distance with the reformers. Though his statements left the door open for a general replacement of Republicans with deserving Democrats, in practice there was no wholesale dismissal of Republicans. He even reappointed a few unusually able Republican officeholders, especially in New York and Massachusetts where the civil service crusaders were most active. During the first six months the reformers were relatively satisfied. Godkin praised Cleveland, and the National Civil Service Reform League took occasion at its convention in August to laud the President for his courageous efforts "amid immense perplexities and difficulties."

Soon thereafter the chorus of reformers began to sound some sour notes. It became apparent that Cleveland, when forced to make a choice, was more interested in the Democratic party than in the Reform League. Reformers were displeased over his refusal to make public specific reasons for the removal of individual Republican officeholders. Early in February, 1886, Carl Schurz implored Cleveland to take the public into his confidence: admit to the public that "in the confusion of the beginning of your administration some removals have been made, much against your intention, which were not in accord with that pledge" to retain all worthy incumbents in office. He also advised him to "issue an executive order that henceforth in every case of removals the reasons therefore shall be put on public record." Two weeks later, the National Civil Service Reform League adopted a resolution expressing Schurz's views on removals.

Reformers watched over patronage matters like hawks and passed up no opportunity to inform Cleveland, directly and indirectly, of spoilsman practices in various states. They kept reminding him of their services in the 1884 campaign and of the importance of this cause to civilization. Richard Rogers Bowker, editor of *Publishers' Weekly,* complained to Cleveland about "the condition of things in Indiana and Philadelphia." He decried the bad appointments that Senator Gorman brought about in his Maryland constituency and charged that this 1884 campaign manager "had kept decidedly bad faith with his political allies."

Schurz explained to Cleveland, in February, 1886, that some of the critics were extremely unjust, "for they overlook the great good you have really accomplished." Schurz considered it the "kind of injustice to which those who are trying to work out difficult reforms are frequently exposed, for even well meaning people are apt to be more mindful of bad things near them than of good things farther away." In Schurz's opinion the critics, on the other hand, were not wholly wrong, for there was "the danger of reform administrations to sit down between two chairs — going far enough to exasperate the opponents of reform, but not far enough to satisfy the bulk of its friends." But by mid-1886 the most the Mugwumps were able to say was that Cleveland had made fewer changes in the civil service personnel than had some Republican Presidents and that he had tried to select the best Democrats. There was no denying Senator George F. Hoar's charge, early that summer, that of the 3,500 positions under Cleveland's immediate control, the President had already nominated over 2,000 Democrats. Statistics on the entire civil service were similar, so that by the end of the presidential term there were relatively few Republicans still in appointive offices. The *Civil*

Service Record observed that it was "not altogether a clean sweep."

The acceleration in the administration's replacement of Republican officeholders with "deserving" Democrats was the result of two developments. The administration's removal and appointive machinery, following a period of slowness imposed by inexperience, indecision and caution, finally began to operate smoothly and rapidly. More important, patronage-hungry Democrats relentlessly put pressure on Cleveland to function definitely as a member of the Democratic party. Fellow Democrats told him, in effect, that on matters involving politics he was bound to perform as a Democrat. To these men the civil service reformers were a flock of chattering magpies who had best be ignored or they would ruin the Democratic party.

The loudest clamor for patronage came from Democratic Congressmen. They believed, and with good reason, that they held their jobs at the sufferance of party men back home. The party workers and financial contributors who had sent them to Washington expected to share in the distribution of the patronage. It would be unthinkable for Congressmen to inform loyal party cohorts that good Republicans were to remain behind the post office grilles simply because they were good fellows and did not overcharge customers who purchased stamps. There were also good and honest Democrats. One such impatient Congressman was Wisconsin's General Edward S. Bragg. He expected a patronage reward for his dramatic "love him for the enemies he has made" speech at the 1884 convention. In June, 1885, he explained to a Chicago newspaperman that he expected the removal of every Republican postmaster in his Congressional district. He talked freely about the great political influence of small-town postmasters and about his intention to use them to the utmost in this capacity. He was not worried about the danger of "milk-sops" being appointed, for "men who are above making themselves useful in politics don't come to me for recommendations for office." Bragg and most of those elected to Congress realized the importance of the Mugwump contribution to the Cleveland victory at the polls, but they also realized that their own individual futures were tied more to Democratic organizations in their bailiwicks than to the relative handful of "good government" reformers concentrated largely in New York and Massachusetts. It was natural that they complained when Cleveland moved slowly in replacing Republicans with Democrats in appointive offices.

Beginning in midsummer, 1885, however, Cleveland gave definite evidence that he was a party traditionalist and not a civil service reformer. Cleveland and Vilas had already, in May, informed Congressmen that they could bring about the removal of Republican postmasters in their districts by simply informing the Post Office Department that the incumbents in question had engaged in offensive partisan activity while in office. Implementation of this policy was now improved by the resignation in July, because of illness, of civil-service-reform-minded Malcolm Hay, the Assistant Postmaster General in charge of fourth-class postmaster appointments. He was replaced by Adlai Stevenson, an ex-Congressman who understood practical politics. Six weeks later, able and high-minded Congressman William L. Wilson, from West Virginia, wrote in his diary that "this has been a great relief to the members." Wilson praised Stevenson for being "naturally prompt, energetic, and accommodating," whereas Hay's "reluctance to make removals except upon strong and compelling evidence, made our work very slow and burdensome."

Although the removal of Republican officeholders cleared the patronage path for the oncoming Democrats, Cleveland strove valiantly to keep undesirable Democrats from getting close to the public trough. Wherever possible, he passed over both professional machine bosses and economic reformers and rewarded instead the Bourbon element. Sometimes they were obscure Bourbons, and sometimes they were Bourbons tinged with bossism, but always they were Bourbons.

Chicago's colorful Mayor Carter H. Harrison, for example, received no plums. He had worked hard for the nomination and election of Cleveland, but he was also commander of a political machine and something of a demagogue. In October, 1886, Harrison wired to Cleveland: "Mr. Peter Jene is a first-class man, a sound democrat and honest popular German. I say this in justice to him but I suppose it will kill his chances as my friendship seems fatal in federal atmosphere." Chicago Bourbons, whose wealth and conservatism were much more conspicuous than their popularity with the voters, were the patronage recipients and agents. Cleveland was especially impressed with the lawyer Melville W. Fuller. This Chicago Bourbon declined Cleveland's proffer of a place on the Civil Service Commission, but in 1888 he accepted the post of Chief Justice of the United States Supreme Court.

It was understandable that the Philadelphia *Press* reacted to the appointment by stating that Fuller was the

most obscure man ever appointed Chief Justice, but
the paper might have added that reliance on relatively
unknown men was characteristic of the Cleveland administration. Not only had the Democrats' long absence from
national power kept party leaders from the center of
the stage, but Cleveland tended to favor men whose
political activity did not happen to include courting public favor. As Bourbons they chose, except in the South,
to confine their political work to policy making, naming
candidates and financing campaigns. Most Northern Bourbons saw little likelihood of winning elections and felt
no impelling reason to leave their lucrative professions
or businesses to seek elective offices. In the South and in
the border states, of course, Bourbons did develop powerful vote-controlling organizations and made themselves
well known to the voters.

Although Cleveland had a genuine distaste for professional machine politicians, he could not prevent some of
them from receiving patronage. Senator Gorman, who
was both a Bourbon and a machine politician, had a claim
that could not easily be denied. As the 1884 campaign
manager, he naturally expected to control patronage in
his home state of Maryland. Cleveland acknowledged his
claim. The result was the appointment of some undesirable persons, one of whom, Baltimore Postmaster I. Parker
Veazey, soon came under fire and wisely resigned.

Cleveland was even more determined and more successful in denying places to claimants tinged with agrarian
reform. He was surrounded with Bourbon advisers more
inclined to make concessions to urban bosses than to
agrarian champions. Agrarian leaders were in no position to force concessions. The state and national party

machinery and the governmental appointive offices were staffed with their determined opponents. Genuine agrarian Democrats in Congress were too few to protest. Vice-President Hendricks, who was very popular among currency reformers in Indiana and among likeminded farmers elsewhere, was not invited to the patronage banquet. He had been very useful for campaign purposes, but the time had now come to purify the party and build it on the solid, undefiled rock of economic conservatism. Hendricks might have joined in the party revolt in later years, if he had not died in 1885, early in his career as Vice-President.

The most dramatic patronage episode was staged in Minnesota, but the forces that gave rise to it were the same almost everywhere in the Democratic party. In addition to the usual city-country cleavage, to the pressure of the restless farmers on one side and of the Bourbons on the other, there was the personal conflict of the colorful antimonopolist leader Ignatius Donnelly against the triumvirate consisting of railroad magnate James J. Hill, national Democratic committeeman Patrick H. Kelly, and the chairman of the Democratic state central committee, Michael Doran. Both Kelly and Doran were Irish-born citizens of the heavily Irish-American and heavily Democratic city of St. Paul, and both were successful businessmen.

The trouble began when Donnelly took steps to collect his reward for the considerable 1884 campaign effort he had made for a Democratic victory. Unquestionably his truly impressive oratorical ability and his long-standing popularity among farmers had done much to increase the normally small Democratic vote in rural areas. Given the opportunity, he might well have been able eventually to turn Minnesota into a Democratic state. He was, in any case, ambitious to become the Democratic leader, and he serenely expected that his services to the party and his friendly relations during the campaign with the highly placed Vilas would net him the minor but politically strategic position of Surveyor General for his state and postmasterships for a few associates. It did not occur to him that there might be some truth in the early post-election observation of a fellow antimonopolist friend: "Cleveland is elected . . . yet I do not look for much relief for the masses, for the same monopolies that run the Republican party run the Democratic party."

Hill was not happy about Donnelly's oratorical efforts, and he was in a position to do something about them without public knowledge. Doran told a reporter that "Mr. Hill isn't in politics." Back during the 1884 campaign Hill had asked Tilden about Cleveland and then proceeded to instruct his railroad officials to work for Cleveland and to send a check for $5000 to the national campaign headquarters. When the time came to check-mate Donnelly, Hill simply left it to his willing cohorts Kelly and Doran, although he wrote enough to Cleveland's secretary, Lamont, to make it clear that he was closely allied with the two on patronage matters. The outcome was that Donnelly received no appointment, and the Minnesota Democracy emerged as a simon-pure Bourbon organization.

Thus, as the months stretched onward, it became apparent that Cleveland took seriously the keynote of his inaugural address — "reform in the administration of the government, and the application of business principles to public affairs." He had made some administrative mistakes and some concessions to machine politicians, but to such a limited extent that relatively few citizens cared. Cleveland's reliance on respectable Bourbons and his own careful scrutiny of job applications protected the nation quite effectively from undesirable officeholders. The record was not great enough to inspire great enthusiasm. But Cleveland and his aides did as well as could be expected in fighting off the horde of poorly qualified, job-hungry party hacks. They were even more successful and more assiduous in screening out all job seekers who showed signs of agrarian or wage-earner radicalism. This purge eventually had a profound effect on the Democratic party and the nation. But meanwhile the Bourbons continued on their course with self-satisfied serenity.

V I
Reluctant Reformer

THOUGH Cleveland provided firm leadership of the administrative branch of the government and of the Democratic party organization, he had difficulties in dealing with aggressive groups in both branches of Congress and with their political allies. After two years of defensive action, he took the offensive. Reluctantly he assumed command of the Democrats in Congress and carried them with him through the 1888 presidential election campaign. In the final accounting, he proved to have fumbled his way to a record of commendable achievement. By the end of his four-year term he had restored some of the prestige lost to the Presidency and to presidential election campaigns by his predecessors during the previous two decades.

From the outset Cleveland and the Republican Senate battled over prerogatives. Ever since the triumph over President Andrew Johnson in the struggle for control of Southern Reconstruction, the Senate had dominated the national political scene. No President had had the temerity to question that control. The Republican Senators were even less considerate of a Democratic President, and they had a special antagonism toward Cleveland and his cohorts. Republican leaders had been defeated in the 1884 election by what they thought to be a band of scheming Democrats who had hoodwinked many Republicans into voting for the "good government" cause. The Senators were bent upon using every opportunity to demonstrate that Cleveland was not a pure reformer. They also hoped the disillusioned Mugwumps would return to the Republican fold.

The fight began early in 1886, when Republican Senators sought to demonstrate that Cleveland was not fulfilling his pledge to remove from office only those officials who had proved inefficient or dishonest or had demonstrated offensive partisanship. When dismissed officials complained that they had been removed in violation of Cleveland's pledge, the Republican Senators went into action.

The Tenure of Office Act, which Congress had enacted in 1867 against President Andrew Johnson, had been later substantially modified to meet the objections of President Grant. In its revised form, it scarcely hampered a determined President in dismissals and appointments of personnel. Nevertheless, the Republican Senators boldly used the Tenure of Office Act to threaten Cleveland. They also attempted to obtain from the executive branch information that Cleveland considered private and confidential. The Senators claimed that it was necessary that they should have access to all information in possession of the executive departments in order to perform their constitutional duties. They reasoned that if Cleveland refused to accede he would create the public impression that he had something to hide. If, on the other hand, he did yield, it would demonstrate that he was partisan in patronage matters. But Cleveland flatly refused to comply.

There was drama in the contest. It was the first opportunity in two decades for the public to watch a clash between a Democratic President and a Republican Senate. In response to senatorial demands for information, Cleveland set forth the constitutional role of the President regarding dismissals and appointments. The Republican Senators, confronted with an increasingly adverse public opinion, standing on untenable legal grounds and lacking real power, finally broke ranks and in the spring of 1886 gave up the fight. Within a year Congress actually repealed what was left of the Tenure of Office Act. More important for the future was Cleveland's emphatic, precedent-making defense of the executive branch's constitutional right to withhold all information of a private or confidential nature and to decide which material was to be so classified. This was also a personal and political victory. The episode underscored Cleveland's reputation for steadfast refusal to be intimidated. At the same time it left him free to interpret as he chose his pledge to retain in office all worthy Republican officials.

Civil service reformers were worried and for good reason. Carl Schurz and the National Civil Service Reform League agreed with Cleveland that he had the constitutional right to withhold private information from Congress, but they also felt that he should tell the public directly why he fired some officeholders. Nevertheless, most voters were so impressed with Cleveland's defiance of the longstanding arrogance of the Senate that they failed to notice, or to care, whether he was fulfilling his pledge regarding removals.

Meanwhile, the contestants engaged in a controversy that fanned into flame the dying Civil War embers. This battle pointedly revealed the emotional climate of the era and the political ineptitude of Cleveland and his Bourbon followers. It also influenced the outcome of the 1888 presidential election. When Cleveland assumed office, he considered the old animosity between the North and South simply nonsense and assumed that most people thought likewise. In his inaugural address he confidently expressed hope that the citizenry would "cheerfully and honestly abandon all sectional prejudice and distrust, and determine, with manly confidence in one another, to work out harmoniously the achievements of our national destiny." There seemed to be justification for his hope. A surprisingly large number of Civil War veterans had voted Democratic in the 1884 election, and early in Cleveland's administration it was apparent that most Northerners gracefully accepted the presence in his Cabinet of ex-Confederates Lamar and Garland and considered it natural and just for many Southerners to receive jobs on the federal payroll.

There were, nevertheless, men aplenty who waited watchfully for opportunities to wave the remnants of the "bloody shirt." Many Republican members of Congress and many Republicans in the Civil War veterans' Grand Army of the Republic were on the alert. They were bent upon demonstrating that the Republican party and the G.A.R. were the only true friends of the veterans and the only true protectors of the cause for which the North had fought and bled.

Patronage and pensions were the initial vehicles of the G.A.R. and their Republican allies. They complained loudly that Cleveland failed to go far enough in applying the principle of veteran preference in removals and appointments: he had confined the practice to disabled veterans. They complained even more when Cleveland used his veto power to check the flood of private pension bills in Congress. They turned deaf ears to his suggestion that the pension system be made fairer, more efficient and more honest. They became increasingly vehement when Cleveland's irritability led him, foolishly, to speak sarcastically in his messages that accompanied vetoed private pension bills. It was not pleasant to have it pointed out that they had voted for bills based on fraudulent claims.

The pension fever in Congress did not end with Cleveland's veto of private bills. It became intense enough to bring about passage, early in 1887, of a long-pending bill that offered pensions to all disabled veterans who had served honorably for at least ninety days and were dependent upon their own efforts for support. Disabilities from old age and other nonmilitary causes were to suffice as qualifications for the stipend. Also included in this "Pauper's Bill" were dependent parents of soldiers who had died in the service. Cleveland vetoed the measure. He said it was wrong to give mere charity seekers an opportunity to receive support from the government, and he reminded Congress of the great burden on the Treasury it would involve.

In the pension skirmish with Congress Cleveland nevertheless sustained a net loss. His vetoes of private pension bills did save a few dollars and did advertise the need for reform. Likewise, he further entrenched his popularity with the segment of the citizenry which already shared his acute indignation at wasteful and dishonest practices. But he failed in his awkward attempts to induce Congress to enact corrective legislation, and the pension problem remained when he left office. He failed politically, for his vetoes helped the Republicans advance their popularity with veterans and with all those susceptible to the appeal of the "bloody shirt." Furthermore, the truculent, uncompromising manner of both the Republican leaders and Cleveland revived the North-South cleavage. Hope for the harmony of which Cleveland spoke in his inaugural address began to dim.

When it was all too apparent that Cleveland should tread cautiously, he stepped squarely into almost every hornets' nest of Civil War memories which a more agile politician, with a little luck, might have avoided. In 1887 Cleveland accepted an invitation to be the guest of St. Louis on the occasion of the national encampment of the G.A.R. in that city. The political element was clearly a factor in both the invitation and its acceptance. Democrats controlled the committee that extended the invitation. It was composed of eight G.A.R. officers, five former Confederates and five civilians. Cleveland, with his eye on the 1888 presidential campaign, welcomed this opportunity to counteract the bad impression his vetoes of pension bills had made among veterans. He also wished to make a personal appearance in the West.

The political factor came to the forefront after the White House announcement that the President preferred a public to a private reception in St. Louis, so that everyone might shake his hand. Thereupon the *National Tribune*, violently pro-Republican G.A.R. organ, launched a crusade against him, and soon the entire press of the nation entered the fray. The editor of the *National Trib-*

une asked: "Does anyone want the National Encampment running in conjunction with a grand political mass meeting?" Several G.A.R. chapters threatened to boycott the encampment, and others passed resolutions warning that Cleveland would be insulted if he attended.

Just when moderate G.A.R. leaders seemed to be successful in their appeals for more dignified regard for the high office of the Presidency, Cleveland made another misstep. This time, Secretary of War Endicott, with the political naïveté so characteristic of Cleveland's entourage, decided it would be a fine gesture of good will toward the South to carry out the suggestion of the Adjutant General to return captured Confederate flags to their former owners. Cleveland, apparently dealing with the matter in routine fashion, gave his approval verbally. Republican Senator Joseph B. Foraker of Ohio, who faced a re-election contest, pounced upon the plan as a means to capture votes. He attacked Cleveland and the Democrats with astounding violence. He called upon the voters to restore the Republicans to power in order "to check the revival of the Southern Confederacy." Cleveland's actions, Foraker proclaimed, revealed the presence of a scheme for Southern dominance. Throughout the North, extremists took up the cry. The Commander in Chief of the Grand Army, Lucius Fairchild of Wisconsin, trembling with excitement over the flag order as he addressed a Harlem Grand Army post, burst forth with: "May God palsy the brain that conceived it, and may God palsy the tongue that dictated it!"

Cleveland soon recognized that it had been a mistake to ignore the existence of sectional prejudice. A legal technicality permitted him to withdraw the order on the battle flags, and he avoided an unfortunate incident by reversing his decision to appear at the Grand Army encampment. Soon, too, the wiser heads in the Grand Army, fearing that Democratic veterans would leave the fold, brought more moderation in that organization. The Republican press also muted its attacks, recognizing that the public showed definite signs of reaction against the extremists.

The veterans' pension issue, however, remained to plague the Democrats in the 1888 presidential campaign. Pensions meant money, and promises of them offered Grand Army and Republican politicians a far more substantial means to retain veteran support than did the "bloody shirt." Cleveland soon found it relatively safe to exhibit a rather defiant indifference to sectionalism. Extremists could make little capital out of his fishing on Memorial Day or of his promotion of Secretary Lamar to the Supreme Court bench. But the pension issue remained very much alive.

Federal financial policy — currency and tariff — resulted in Cleveland's closest contact with Congress. But he cautiously and skillfully avoided the political explosion inherent in the discussion of currency policy. A crusade for reform of the currency would certainly have involved him in a struggle with a large and determined Democratic majority in the House of Representatives. Cleveland's ideas on finance were Bourbon; and the reform he wanted required legislation not popular in the House, the Democratic majority of which was agrarian.

An episode in February, 1885, a month before his inauguration, showed clearly how very wide was the gulf between Cleveland and the Democratic House. His New

York associates, concerned over the future of the gold
standard, induced the President-elect to urge Congress
to end the continuous addition of silver to the currency
supply that was mandatory under the Bland-Allison Act
of 1878. The unsatisfactory condition of the gold reserve
in the Treasury was the immediate pretext. It had been
generally accepted that the Treasury would have no difficulty redeeming in gold any currency if there was a gold
reserve on hand of at least $100,000,000. That sum was
originally accumulated to support the greenbacks, while
government bonds constituted the collateral which gave
value to the national-bank notes. But after 1878, with the
passage of the Bland-Allison Act, between two and four
million dollars' worth of silver had to be purchased each
month and coined into dollars. The Treasury unofficially
made these silver dollars redeemable in gold, in order to
have all currency on the gold standard. Although there
was actually only eighty-five cents' worth of gold value
in the silver dollars, no problem arose because they were
exchangeable for gold. But if the gold reserve should
dwindle, the entire national financial structure would be
jolted. Persons with title to dollars or investments valued
in terms of dollars therefore kept a close watch on the
Treasury gold reserve and became fearful whenever it
showed signs of diminishing.

On the other hand, a very large number of citizens,
especially farmers of the West and South, wanted more
money in circulation, and they reasoned that situation
could best be achieved by a substantial increase in the
amount of silver currency. Their belief that the currency
supply was inadequate was based on such evidence as the
scarcity of money available for loans to farmers — interest

rates, even based on land mortgages, often being as high as twelve to fifteen per cent. Farmers also argued that a ruinous decline in prices was caused by creeping deflation. Although economic activity and population increased rapidly, there was no corresponding increase in the money supply. This relative increase in the value of money resulted in lower prices for products. There was no such decrease in the supply of wheat, corn, cotton, livestock and other farm products, but there was a gradual decrease in their market value in terms of the rising value of currency. Debtor farmers, of whom there were many, were especially angry. They found themselves selling one and a half or two bushels of wheat to pay debts incurred when one bushel was equivalent to the amount borrowed. Farmers without debt escaped undue hardship, except during depressions, because there was also a decline in the prices of items and services they purchased. But even many of these farmers were angry and embittered because of the hard times of the 1870's and the government policies that discriminated against them.

Against that background of discontent and disagreement, Cleveland was called upon to act even before assuming office. On February 2, 1885, chairman of the House Ways and Means Committee Abram S. Hewitt wrote excitedly to Cleveland that "we are in the presence of great peril." The gold reserve was sliding down close to the danger line — $100,000,000. By February 24, however, gold was again flowing into the Treasury and the crisis was ended. But Tilden, Manning and other Bourbons had already persuaded Cleveland to take a firm and aggressive position. They were clearly less concerned over the immediate condition of the gold reserve than over the possibility of a graver crisis ahead. They wanted definite assurance from Cleveland that a Democratic President would be as adamant a defender of sound money as had been the long line of Republicans. On February 28, Cleveland sent a letter to ninety-five Democratic Congressmen who had petitioned him not to succumb to the Bourbon laments. He requested them to remove the ever-increasing silver dollar pressure on the gold reserve. This, he asserted, could be done by suspending the silver purchase and coinage provision of the Bland-Allison Act. Two days later the House defeated the proposal by a vote of 170 to 118. Only fifty-two Democrats voted on the Bourbon side. Thus, even before the new administration took office, it was perfectly clear that the Bourbon administration and the agrarian-Democratic House were at opposite poles on the currency issue. The Republican Senate, on the other hand, was in harmony with the Bourbons on the matter.

Neither Cleveland nor Congress paid the price necessary for constructive legislation on the currency problem. The cost involved a searching examination of economic conditions, formulation of a new program and ability to lead the citizenry to acceptance of that new approach. That was too high a price for Cleveland, for Congress or for any person or group who appeared conspicuously upon the scene during those years. In this absence of understanding, both Cleveland and his adversaries continued to act and think within the narrow confines of rusty dogmas, piecemeal expedients, idealistic cure-all nostrums and political jockeying.

In both the Cleveland and Congressional approach to the currency aspect of financial policy, political jockeying was most conspicuous. For two years after taking office Cleveland avoided a clash with the silver Congressmen. He made no serious attempt to discipline the House Democrats, permitting political anarchy to prevail in that quarter. The President's reason, or perhaps excuse, for nonintervention in House affairs was based on a literal, ultralegalistic interpretation of the Constitution. Apparently without giving thought to his unique responsibilities and rights as an official elected by the nation as a whole, Cleveland decided that the Constitution restricted his powers to purely executive matters, apart from the right to make recommendations to Congress and to veto bills. He even stated this view publicly and thereby damaged his influence greatly. In January, 1886, when House silverites were actively attempting to commit that body to free and unlimited coinage of silver at a ratio of 16 ounces of silver to 1 ounce of gold, Cleveland escaped involvement in the controversy by informing the press that "this is an executive office." He believed, Cleveland explained, that "the most important benefit that I can confer on the country by my presidency is to insist upon the entire independence of the executive and legislative branches of government, and compel the members of the legislative branch to see that they have responsibilities of their own, grave and well defined, which their official oaths bind them sacredly to perform."

During the 1886 session of Congress the silverites pushed to a vote the Bland bill for free and unlimited coinage of silver at a ratio of 16 to 1. They were beaten 163 to 126. But the free silverites and moderates were able to join forces to defeat a Bourbon attack on the Bland-Allison Act by a vote of 201 to 84. One hundred and sixty-three Democratic votes were on the anti-Bourbon column.

The silver leaders next concentrated on the Treasury surplus and were so successful that it could not escape notice that Cleveland and his Bourbon cohorts had lost control of the situation. Leadership of the Democratic party was fast gravitating toward the silverites. The occasion for this turn of events was passage, in both the House and Senate, of a resolution instructing the Treasury what to do with its surplus income.

Although in early 1885 public and political attention had focused on the precarious state of the gold reserve and the mounting silver reserve, by 1886 the situation was reversed. There was now a large, and rapidly growing, surplus of both gold and silver in the Treasury. From the late 1860's onward, and more markedly since early 1881, the Treasury had been taking in more money than it had paid out (the 1885 decline in the gold reserve having been unique). During fiscal 1886 there was a remarkable growth in government revenue, due especially to an increase of $50,000,000 collected in import duties. The available disposable balance was $75,000,000 compared with $40,000,000 the previous year; $57,000,000 of this surplus was in gold.

A House resolution, introduced by William R. Morrison of Illinois, called for a drastic reduction of this surplus through the purchase and retirement of government bonds. Money would thus be placed in circulation and the taxpayers saved from paying interest on the bonds. The surplus could be used to purchase and retire a portion of the $140,000,000 in bonds then subject to redemption at par value. Cleveland and all gold standard devotees were disturbed by the proposal. Because it provided for disposal of the entire surplus above the $100,000,000 reserve, no leeway would remain to meet possible emergencies. In short, the sound money defenders believed that a reserve of $100,000,000 was too small.

Cleveland acted too late and too feebly to check the movement in the House. On July 14, in a letter to Congressman Samuel J. Randall, he was apologetic. "You know," he wrote, "that I am not at all inclined to meddle with proposed legislation while pending in Congress. My object in sending this is to express in writing, to avoid all misunderstanding, my regret that any of our friends in the House should deem it necessary to aid in such legislation as is contemplated by the resolution now pending." He was, he added, "unable to see why the Treasury Department should not be trusted as previously it has been, under other Administrations." On the same day the House passed the measure and sent it to the Senate. There, although it was modified sufficiently to make it no menace to the gold standard, its passage by a vote of forty-two to twenty was evidence that Congress was legislating in a manner and direction not in line with Cleveland's ideas. The measure died in conference, but it jogged the administration into using more of the surplus to retire government bonds.

During the same session a House majority also disregarded Cleveland's wishes on tariff reduction. Early in June Cleveland interviewed Democratic Congressmen unfriendly to Morrison's tariff bill. Two weeks later a roll-call vote was taken on the measure and the result was defeat by a vote of 170 to 140. Protectionist Randall and thirty-four other Democrats had defied the wishes of the party majority and the President. An unnamed Democratic Congressman told a correspondent for the Democratic New York *Herald:* "It is a black eye for the President, and I for my part am not sorry for him. If he had not declared in January that he took no interest in the silver suspension question he could have carried that. He chose to go back on his policy in that matter, and he ought to have kept out of this tariff business." The irate Congressman added: "A President of the United States ought to have great influence with his party, but Mr. Cleveland deliberately threw his away, and he can't now pick it up again."

In August Congress adjourned, and its members turned their attention to the mid-term election. Cleveland prepared for a bit of fishing and cogitation. In December, when Congress returned to Washington, it discovered a change in the President. He threatened to call an extra session if Congress failed to carry out his recommendations for suspension of silver purchases and reduction of tariff duties. House leaders managed to bring the Morrison tariff bill to a vote but were defeated 154 to 169. On the currency question no measure reached the voting stage. Hence, when Congress adjourned in March, 1887, Cleveland was left in a precarious position, both as head of his party and chief of state. Party members had again rebuffed him, and his effectiveness as President was deteriorating because of the increasingly critical currency surplus in the Treasury.

During the ensuing nine months Cleveland took note of his predicament and then acted with dramatic boldness. As the surplus continued to expand, the financial situation deteriorated, and the public increasingly despaired over the absence of leadership. With the close of 1887 the only available means of disposing of the surplus — reduction of the national debt through redemption of maturing government bonds — would end. During the fiscal year 1888 the Treasury would accumulate an undisposable surplus (above the required $100,000,000) of $125,000,000 — or one twelfth of the total circulation of the nation's currency. "It is mere confession of ignorance," said Professor Henry C. Adams, "to say that a contraction of currency equal to one-twelfth of its amount within a year can do no harm to trade." Adams believed "it would tend to bring about a stringent money market, and would probably precipitate a commercial crisis."

Many plans for spending the money circulated. But each contained political dynamite; most were unorthodox, and some too remindful of the pork barrel to arouse Cleveland's enthusiasm. There were suggestions to distribute the funds to banks to swell their lending capacity; to give them as pensions for war veterans; to purchase the telegraph business; to subsidize steamships; to develop internal waterways and harbors; to aid education; to retire state debts; to create national forests; to retire the greenbacks; to construct post offices and other public buildings; to refund the remainder of the national debt; to repeal the Bland-Allison Act; to reduce the excise taxes on whisky and tobacco; and to lower tariff duties.

Tariff reform impressed Cleveland as the only acceptable approach to the problem, and he proceeded to crusade for it. The intellectual reasons for tariff reduction were at least as compelling as for any other plan; the political pitfalls seemed large, but less so than those of othe proposals.

Cleveland's first step was to ascertain the proper role of the tariff in our national economic system. Before he became President, and apparently until 1886, he knew little about the tariff and had very little interest in it. But the pressing need for action impelled him to become better informed. His Cabinet was so loaded with tariff reformers that it frightened Democratic protectionist leader Randall. Especially ardent were Bayard and Vilas. In fact, practically all the members of the Bourbon hierarchy in the administration and close to the administration were for lower duties. Most of them were connected with the railroad-banking-merchant segment of the economy, which leaned definitely in the low tariff direction. A few of them, like Bayard, were old-time doctrinaire Democrats dedicated to the cause. Cleveland's intimate social companions were tariff reformers. Certainly he was not unaware of the low tariff views of such card-playing cronies as Vilas and Congressman William L. Scott of Pennsylvania. It was not difficult for Cleveland to take the first step — becoming convinced that tariff reform was a worthy cause.

The rest was political. He began by conferring with individual politicians and ended by committing the national Democratic party to the cause. Early in September, 1887, he held strategy meetings at his home in suburban Washington. These "Oak View Conferences" were attended chiefly by tariff reform leaders of the House of Representatives — Speaker John G. Carlisle, William L. Scott, Roger Q. Mills and others. There also was Secretary of the Treasury Charles S. Fairchild, who had held that position since Manning's resignation early in the year because of illness. There was talk at the conferences about the general nature of the proposed tariff measure and the assignment of Mills and Carlisle to the preparation of the bill, with the aid of Fairchild. Cleveland made it clear to the conferees and to the watching public that he intended to work actively to get a tariff measure adopted.

At the same time it became apparent that Cleveland needed to demonstrate unequivocal positiveness in his bid to achieve leadership of his party and to escape a record of failure in the critical surplus problem, for protectionist Democrats would certainly attempt to prevent tariff reform. Ever since the Civil War they had successfully kept their party from conducting any serious tariff reform crusade; and they felt confident that they could still prevent the party from unifying behind the movement. The initial test of strength would be in the House, with the Cleveland forces pitted against the Democratic protectionists and the cooperating Republicans. It would not be easy for Cleveland to reverse the situation. It was too late to wield the patronage whip, for these men had long since had the post offices in their constituencies filled with their followers. Cleveland's only hope was to go over their heads to the 1888 election campaign. If he could commit the national party organization to tariff reform and create the impression that the party had a good chance for victory at the polls, he would be in a commanding position. Loyalty to the party and fear of the party whip were his strongest assets.

Cleveland had either to surrender or push forward — and he pushed forward. He chose the regular annual message of the President as his instrument. During November Cleveland labored over the document, and on

December 1 he presented a preview of the finished product to his Cabinet. Whitney, and some other members, advised him against such an uncompromising stand on the eve of a national election. Ever conscious of the strategic New York electoral vote, Whitney feared the message would cost Cleveland at least that state in the 1888 election. But true to his nature, Cleveland had made up his own mind and would not retreat. On December 8 the message went to Congress.

Having made the basic decision to act forthrightly, Cleveland then made an impressive bid for political unity of the Democratic party and at the same time demonstrated a sense of responsibility toward the nation as a whole. Especially striking was his political tactic of confining the entire message to one item — the tariff. It was the first time that a President had devoted his entire "state of the Union" message to one topic. This break with tradition insured nationwide attention to the issue and emphasized Cleveland's leadership. With the eyes of the voters now focused on the tariff, on Cleveland and on the Democratic party, it was politically impossible for the party to sidetrack the issue.

The message itself was moderate in tone and cleverly conceived. Cleveland carefully avoided commitment to either free trade or protectionism and thereby attempted to escape definite identification with extremists. "Our progress toward a wise conclusion," he said, "will not be improved by dwelling upon the theories of protection and free-trade. This savors too much of bandying epithets." Then, in a sentence that was to be widely quoted, Cleveland asserted: "It is a *condition* which confronts us, not a theory."

The reform he advocated reflected economic and social enlightenment as well as political acumen. He cast aside the proposals for the reduction of excise taxes on tobacco and whisky and of import duties on luxuries. He confined his demands to reduction of duties on the necessities of life and on the raw materials used in the manufacture of necessities. He attempted to explain to laborers and farmers how they would benefit through lower prices, and he tried to allay the worst fears of manufacturers and their employees by assurances that sufficient duties would be retained for protection.

Cleveland showed impressive political canniness in his selection and treatment of specific aspects of the tariff. Certainly there was shrewd calculation in his detailed discussion of the effect of tariff duties on wool and manufactured woolen goods. Wool was produced in Indiana (and of course elsewhere) and woolens were manufactured in New England. Both places were of special political importance. Always in presidential elections the parties fought desperately to capture the large electoral vote of doubtful Indiana, which received almost as much attention as New York State. Cleveland demonstrated with statistics and logic that tariff reform would save the woolgrowers more money on the goods they purchased than they would lose by the lower price received for the raw wool they marketed. New England was currently the area receiving, perhaps overoptimistically, most attention by the tariff reformers. In 1887 Congressman William L. Wilson of West Virginia and House Speaker Carlisle had journeyed to Boston to lecture on tariff reform and were well received; Mugwump tariff reformers in the region were working assiduously to convert their neighbors. New

England manufacturers were smarting and bleeding from the high duties on raw materials — wool, coal, copper, iron ore and scrap metal. Cleveland's emphasis on reduction, or even elimination, of duties on raw materials, with wool used as an example, was certainly done with one eye cast hopefully toward New England.

Cleveland made cautious reference to the relationship between high tariff duties and monopoly. He said: ". . . it is notorious that . . . competition . . . is too often strangled by combinations quite prevalent at this time, and frequently called trusts, which have for their object the regulation of the supply and price of commodities made and sold by members of the combination." In this instance, as with his endorsement in the same year of the Interstate Commerce Commission measure, Cleveland showed that he was cognizant of the problem. But his approach to it was much more hesitant than that of the rapidly growing Farmers' Alliance and of such individuals as Henry George and Henry Demarest Lloyd. He clearly had no intention of becoming intimately associated with the increasing antimonopoly agitation.

The nation's reception of Cleveland's performance was marked by striking contrasts. Except with persons who felt that their economic or political well-being was endangered the public reacted favorably. His action seemed to confirm the belief that Cleveland placed the nation's interest above his own and that of selfish persons in his party.

The practical politicians, whose special interest was vote counting, were not impressed. Democratic professionals were glum; Republican professionals were gleeful. Both groups felt that Cleveland had already acquired

the maximum of supporters through exhibition of ex-
alted public interest morality and that his blunt tariff
stand was certain to lose more votes than it would gain
for the Democracy. The results of the mid-term 1886
election had been indecisive, but they had indicated that
the Democracy had a reasonable chance for victory in
1888 if no crisis developed. Now Cleveland seemed to
have created that crisis.

The tariff message and the entire record of the Cleveland administration were presented to the voters for
judgment in the 1888 election. It was the first time in a
generation or more that a national Democratic administration had been called upon to defend its record; and it
was the first time in the same period that it had seemed
to have something definite to offer — tariff reform. The
voters would now have a better opportunity than usual
to participate meaningfully in the democratic process and
to add impetus to both good government and economic
reform. But it became all too apparent that Cleveland
had driven his party onto higher ground than it was
capable of holding. The Democratic reform leadership
faltered and then scattered.

The most conspicuous failure was that of Cleveland
himself. Cleveland possessed the personal qualities to command but not to lead. More was required of him than to
make pronouncements and issue orders. After instructing
House leaders to pass a new tariff bill, he allowed them to
formulate and to pass one that was manifestly unsatisfactory. Known as the Mills bill, because its chief archi-
tect was Congressman Roger Q. Mills of Texas, it had
the fatal political weakness of being designed for popularity where popularity was least needed and was certain

to arouse antagonism where opposition would be most costly. Its provisions favored the Democratic South, invited anger in strategic Indiana and other wool-growing states and closed the door against possible substantial Democratic gains in New England. The very slight reduction on the sugar duty favored Louisiana, on pig iron the foundries of Alabama and Tennessee; and the lack of reduction on bituminous coal and iron ore favored the various Southern mining states. The unchanged duty on rice pleased South Carolina. Little revision was provided for Southern-made low-grade cotton goods, but most of the protection to Northern-made woolen textiles was eliminated. The North faced heavy reductions on finished metal products, wool, glass, starch and crockery, and the inclusion on the free list of copper ore, tin plate, flax, hemp, lumber, salt and the very important item — wool. Otherwise it was a moderate measure, reducing the average duties about five per cent from the existing forty-seven and thereby reducing the Treasury receipts a contemplated $50,000,000. Cleveland was not pleased with this measure reflecting Southern sectionalism, but he waited too long to prevent its introduction and passage.

In June, before the vote was taken that passed the Mills bill in the House, the Democrats held their national convention. Cleveland's preparations for the gathering showed that he had become concerned about the political dangers of the tariff question. Not only was the Mills bill politically bad, but the Republicans had been carrying on a devastating cannonade against Cleveland's tariff message that worried him. They kept reiterating that it was a bid for free trade and a surrender to the interests of Irish-persecuting England. Cleveland had failed to foresee fully such attacks when planning his 1887 tariff message, and now he was nervous about the effect the Republican charges might have on the voters. He decided it would be politically wise if the 1888 Democratic convention and the campaign managers de-emphasized the tariff issue.

Realizing that he must at all costs avoid giving the appearance of a personal retreat, Cleveland recruited the aid of Gorman, the Maryland Senator who was both a skillful political manipulator and a high tariff advocate. Cleveland wrote out his views in the form of a platform and then asked Gorman to bend every effort to obtain its adoption at the convention. At the convention Gorman easily enlisted the help of Randall, who approved of the tariff plank in the draft but was not told it was written by Cleveland. The ardent tariff reformers, led by editor Henry Watterson of the Louisville *Courier-Journal,* fought valiantly for a more positive reform. They believed this was in keeping with the wishes of Cleveland. Gorman found it necessary to retreat to the position that the other delegates *supposed* was Cleveland's position. But in actuality the closest Cleveland wanted the convention to get to the tariff question was to exhume and reaffirm the innocuous 1884 party platform. The Cleveland draft began with: "The democratic Party of the United States in national Convention assembled, renews the pledge of its fidelity to Democratic faith, and reaffirms the platform adopted by its representatives in the Convention of 1884." To this, the Watterson group succeeded in adding: "and endorses the views expressed by President Cleveland in his last earnest message to Congress as the correct interpretation of that platform upon the question of tariff reduction; and also endorsed the efforts of our Democratic representatives in Congress to secure a reduction of excessive taxation." On the Mills bill, which Gorman and also Senator Charles J. Faulkner of West Virginia later insisted Cleveland wanted the platform to ignore, the convention adopted a separate resolution calling for its passage.

Another evidence of Cleveland's desire to retreat on the issue was his endorsement of nontariff reform and antitariff reform men for conspicuous roles in the campaign. The closest exception to that pattern was the nomination of Ohio's Senator Allen G. Thurman for the Vice-Presidency. This aged and infirm Old Roman, as he was lovingly called by a host of devoted Democrats, was not an enthusiastic tariff reformer. Even more ridiculous was the selection of William H. Barnum of Connecticut and Calvin S. Brice of Ohio to manage the national campaign. Chairman Barnum, chosen by Cleveland upon the advice of Gorman, was a high tariff advocate. He owned large areas of iron ore, and as a member of the Iron and Steel Association was closely allied with ardent protectionists. In 1886 he led a fight to destroy the tariff reform movement in Connecticut. Brice, chairman of the executive committee, was a wealthy lawyer and railroad entrepreneur, with obvious protectionist views. Later, when he was in the Senate, he fought tariff reduction. It was not surprising that their efforts to spread the gospel of tariff reform during the campaign were something less than halfhearted. The "campaign of education" on the issue would have been sorry indeed without the efforts of individual reformers of such independent organizations as the Free Trade League, the Massachusetts Tariff

Reform League and the American Tariff Reform League.
Candidate Cleveland's campaign effort was almost completely negative. He took the position that it would be undignified for him to campaign. He also kept the Cabinet members at their desks in Washington until late in the campaign. Only once, in his letter accepting the nomination, did he expose his thoughts to the public; and then it was with a mildness in startling contrast to his celebrated 1887 tariff message. This time the occasion called for a rousing political call to arms. But when finally issued in September his approach was cautious rather than dynamic. On the tariff, as in his 1887 message, he confined himself almost entirely to oblique attack on the current tariff rates — concentrating on the Treasury surplus problem instead of the monopoly-breeding aspect of excessive tariff duties. While composing the message, he nevertheless gave some thought to the great advantage that high duties afforded the manufacturers. In one longhand draft he wrote: "The increase of price added by the duty to foreign importations permits our home dealers and manufacturers to charge for their domestic goods of the same kind, though burdened with no tariff duty, prices at least approximating those charged for the goods competing with theirs which have paid such duty." He crossed out that sentence and replaced it with: "I suppose, too, it is well understood that the effect of this tariff taxation is not limited to the consumers of imported articles, but that the duties upon such articles permit a corresponding increase in price to be laid upon domestic productions of the same kind." The message was in this latter form when Cleveland submitted a draft to his Cabinet for criticism, and it remained that way

following their scrutiny. Tied as he was to the Bourbon element in the Democracy, he was prevented from launching a broad attack on monopoly. He was not free nor personally inclined to join forces with irate anti-monopolist farm leaders and intellectual devotees of the Manchester school of economics. The excited crusaders, who employed such terms as the tariff being the "mother of trusts," also had some thoughts about the excesses of railroad and money monopolies which were not curable by tariff reduction.

Throughout the campaign Cleveland worried about the possible consequences of his 1887 tariff message, and when the campaign was over he continued to worry. A statement to his friend William B. Hornblower seemed either to apologize or to defend himself for his recklessness. Hornblower reported that when he called at the White House a few days after the election, Cleveland seemed to have his tariff message on his mind: " 'My friends all advised me not to send it in. They told me that it would hurt the party; that without it, I was sure to be re-elected, but that if I sent in that message to Congress, it would in all probability defeat me; that I could wait till after election and then raise the tariff question. I felt, however, that this would not be fair to the country; the situation as it existed to my mind was intolerable and immediate action was necessary. Besides, I did not wish to be re-elected without having the people understand just where I stood on the tariff question and then spring the question on them after my re-election.' He paused a moment and then added, as if speaking to himself: 'Perhaps I made a mistake from the party standpoint; but damn it, it was right,' and he brought his fist down on his desk, 'I have at least that satisfaction.' "

The defenders of high tariff duties evidenced much more zeal, unity and acumen than the low tariff forces. The Republican party and various organizations of industrialists conducted spirited attacks. In June, at the Republican national convention, the high protectionists pushed aside the tariff reform element in their party. They nominated Benjamin Harrison of Indiana for the Presidency and Levi Morton of New York for the Vice-Presidency. Both men were known ultraprotectionists. In the Senate, meanwhile, the Allison bill was debated. In this tariff measure, drawn up by Senators William B. Allison of Iowa, Nelson W. Aldrich of Rhode Island and Frank Hiscock of New York, provision was made for a $70,000,000 revenue reduction. The duties on sugar were to be halved, many items not produced in this country placed on the free list, and the excise tax on tobacco abolished. The high duties on necessities were retained. Thus, while the general consumer might be offended, many farmers, miners and factory communities would be relieved of much worry. The Allison bill also had the shrewdly devised advantage of undercutting the chief reason advanced by Cleveland for tariff reduction — the surplus. The party platform declared that "we favor the entire repeal of internal taxes, rather than the surrender of any part of our protective system."

During the campaign, able orators, newspapers and a flood of pamphlets spread the "information" that the Democrats were free trade slaves of England, were willing to expose the workingmen to the competition of lower-paid workers abroad by placing the products they made on the same price level and were willing to accept the ruination of American farms and factories. Candidate Harrison made a series of ninety-four brief, effective and thoughtful tariff speeches to delegations that came to him in Indianapolis. In October the Republicans cleverly bid for Western farm support in particular and for the support of the moderates in general by permitting passage in the Senate of the Allison bill.

Democratic halfheartedness and bungling and Republican zeal and skill extended to other aspects of the campaign. Many Democratic party workers simply did not like Cleveland as their candidate, and consequently they did not work diligently for his election. At the convention the mention of Horatio Seymour and Samuel J. Tilden brought louder cheers from the delegates than did the name Cleveland. Friends of the President attributed this solely to the spoilsmen who resented Cleveland's partiality to the businessmen-Bourbons rather than to the professional bosses in patronage distribution. But many Democrats who were not machine politicians simply resented Cleveland's manner and his actions. They had discovered that the socially jolly, modest, storytelling Cleveland was politically very difficult to get along with. He often treated politicians in a suspicious manner, showed resentment or impatience if they disagreed with him, was often blindly stubborn and occasionally downright vindictive. Frequently the performance of these politicians deserved Cleveland's disfavor, but his manner did not add to their liking for him. Cleveland also made it difficult for some politicians to maintain their home political fences, constructed of such materials as promises of government jobs, pensions, currency expansion and tariff protection.

It did not help Cleveland with politicians when he assumed the public pose of a man above and against the sordid game of political maneuvering and, at the same time, not only played politics himself but expected the politicians to pick his chestnuts out of the fire and to carry the burden of his election. Harassed politicians, conscious of the popular impression that "all politicians are crooked," did not feel drawn to Cleveland when he seemed ostentatiously to parade his own honesty as though it were unique. This quality in Cleveland caused such stories to circulate as the one regarding his remark upon learning that his young son Richard prevented himself from getting a perfect mark on a school assignment by pointing out an error in his work that his teacher had overlooked. Cleveland said that the boy seemed to be taking after his father, "because untruthfulness appears to be no temptation whatever to either of us."

Many loyal followers of Tilden (who had died in 1886) felt that Cleveland had not shown proper deference to the great leader nor to his devoted lieutenant Manning (who had died in January, 1887). In New York State especially the Tilden group was markedly hostile toward Cleveland. Perhaps they expected an undue amount of deference from Cleveland, but he would have been more politic to have demonstrated more gratitude for the Tilden-Manning role in his rise to the Presidency. The result was unfortunate for the 1888 Democratic campaign effort.

Democratic mismanagement and Republican efficiency determined the final outcome. It is doubtful that the tariff issue changed the vote of any state. The Republicans carried both Indiana and New York State and hence the national election.

In Indiana it is possible that it was the extensive Republican bribery that won, but it is just as possible that the exposure of the bribery during the campaign and the brazenness of it lost the Republicans more votes than they acquired. Other factors in the Indiana campaign picture were: an Indianan at the head of the ticket, the tariff, the liquor question, and Civil War veteran pensions. Harrison carried the state by a margin of only 2,300, a fact which proved no more than that each party needed repairs in that key state.

In New York a major factor in the Republican victory was the abysmal lack of harmony in the Democratic party organization. This time there was no Cleveland-Tammany rift. Honest John Kelly had died in 1886, and now at the head of Tammany was the ruthlessly able Richard Croker. Cleveland and Whitney, Cleveland's chief aide on New York political affairs, had managed to get along with Croker. Some patronage to Croker and promises of noninterference in Tammany affairs contributed much to the harmony. In 1886 the pro-Cleveland Democracy and Tammany had successfully joined forces to elect Abram S. Hewitt to the New York mayoralty, in a three-way contest against Theodore Roosevelt and single-taxer Henry George. In 1888 the anti-Cleveland opposition revolved around Democrat David H. Hill, Cleveland's successor in the governorship. Hill was both a brilliant and an ambitious politician and had an impressive following among the Democrats. At the same time, because his methods and principles were highly questionable, he had aroused the wrath of the "good government" element. Cleveland did not approve of him and was more than a little irritated by Hill's maneuvers to dominate the state party and to obtain the presidential nomination.

In 1888 it finally developed that Hill ran for re-election to the governorship and shrewdly gave Cleveland a lukewarm endorsement for the Presidency. But Cleveland, despite the entreaties of Whitney and other advisers, flatly refused to endorse Hill's candidacy. The coldness between these two men resulted in losses to Cleveland of party regulars who looked upon Hill as a purer Democrat. At the same time Cleveland lost ground with Mugwump supporters of the 1884 contest because his name was on the party ticket with a spoilsman. Other elements contributing to the outcome were the coolness of the Tilden-Manning group, the tariff, Civil War veterans' pensions, Republican bribery and the Murchison letter episode. The latter was a cleverly contrived Republican trick to make it seem that Cleveland was unduly friendly toward England and hence disloyal to the Irish and other Anglophobe voters. In New York Harrison won over Cleveland by 13,002, while Democrat Hill won the governorship by a 19,171 plurality.

Nationally the Republicans won by a close vote — carrying Harrison into the Presidency with an electoral vote of 233 to 168, but a minority popular vote. Cleveland had a plurality of over 100,000. The Republicans obtained control of both branches of Congress. The Democrats could take some satisfaction from the majority popular vote for Cleveland and the capture of doubtful New Jersey and Connecticut.

The four-year experiment with Cleveland-Bourbon rule ended on a note of uncertainty. The Cleveland-Bourbon team had worked hard, with a sense of responsibility and with success, to provide the administrative branch of the government with a higher level of decency and efficiency than they had inherited when they assumed command. Politically, Cleveland and the Bourbons seemed somewhat to have rehabilitated the Democratic party. Previously North-South sectionalism had deeply wounded the party, the currency issue had divided it and boss-ridden city machines had robbed it of much of its respectability. Now those blights seemed to be reduced.

The impact of Cleveland's personality on government and politics was his greatest value to the nation. Some of his predecessors of the era had shown as much honesty, independence, stubborn courage, intelligence and understanding. But Cleveland's temperament and decent impulses combined to help him add to the influence of the office of the Presidency and to the power of the headship of a political party. Along the way, ironically, he was at times politically awkward, inconsistent, uncertain and obtuse; and his knowledge and understanding left much to be desired. But those qualities actually contributed toward his success. Combined with his righteous indignation at obstructions in his path, they caused him to go over the heads of Congress, of powerful elements in his party and of pressure groups in general and to place his case before the public. Myths about Cleveland made him seem to be a truly great and unblemished defender of democracy and all its virtues. His actual achievements, together with these myths, served as an inspiration to succeeding political leaders. In later years, more sophisticated Presidents took the same general path but with their superior skill and knowledge achieved a more enduring greatness.

V I I
Cautious Politician

THE DECADE of the 1880's drifted to a close with several public problems still unsolved — chief of them the yet unrelieved economic plight of the farmers and wage earners. A growing number of citizens were convinced that the federal government must inaugurate positive reforms in the tariff, currency-banking and monopoly practices. President Cleveland, whose energies initially had been diverted exclusively toward honesty and efficiency, had finally, in 1887, ventured to tackle the difficult problem of the tariff. But he shunned the task of reforming the currency-banking system or of curbing exploitative monopolies. Except for incidental references to the connection between the tariff and monopoly, Cleveland concentrated his bid for lower import tariff duties on the purely governmental aspect of their relation to the Treasury surplus and federal taxation.

But after his defeat in 1888, the Cleveland who prepared to relinquish his office to Benjamin Harrison suddenly acquired a broader understanding of the national economic structure and a deeper sympathy for those victimized by its faults. Now he spoke with greater emphasis on the degree to which high tariff rates fostered "special privilege" groups to exploit the humble citizen.

The new Cleveland was strikingly revealed in the President's final (December, 1888) message to Congress on the "state of the Union." "The gulf between employers and the employed," said Cleveland, "is constantly widening, and classes are rapidly forming, one comprising the very rich and powerful, while in another are found the toiling poor. As we view the achievements of aggregated capital, we discover the existence of trusts, combinations and monopolies, while the citizen is struggling far in the rear or is trampled to death beneath the iron heel." After referring to the interests that received special favors through the government, particularly in the form of high tariff duties, Cleveland reminded Congress that "the grievances of those not included within the circle of these beneficiaries, when fully realized, will surely arouse irritation and discontent." He predicted that "our farmers, long suffering and patient, struggling in the race of life with hardest and most unremitting toil, will not fail to see, in spite of misrepresentations and misleading fallacies, that they are obliged to accept such prices for their products as are fixed in foreign markets where they compete with the farmers of the world; that their debts increase, and that without compensating favor they are forced by the action of the Government to pay for the benefit of others such enhanced prices for the things they need that the scanty returns of the labor fail to furnish their support or leave no margin for accumulation." Then, turning his attention to another group, Cleveland said that "our workingmen . . . will reasonably demand . . .

steadier employment, cheaper means of living in their homes, freedom for themselves and their children from the doom of perpetual servitude, and an open door to their advancement beyond the limits of a laboring class."

Cleveland's proposed remedy was based on his assumption that unreasonable economic inequality was a result of special privileges. He mentioned the discriminatory nature of the laws governing public and Indian lands, pensions, internal improvements and the tariff — with greatest emphasis on the tariff. He proposed to confine the government to its proper functions as prescribed in the Constitution — which Cleveland believed did not include paternalistic aid to any group or individual.

Unfortunately Cleveland's intellectual growth stopped at that point, and his will to crusade even for his own limited objectives faltered. Though the need for economic reform mounted rapidly, during the ensuing four years Cleveland retreated into the role of a cautious, conservative politician. He remained almost silent or straddled these issues. Only once, in 1891, did he speak forth boldly, and that was to castigate the free silverites, while offering an olive branch to the moderate bimetallists. Clearly he was seeking re-election to the Presidency in 1892, and clearly he believed his best chance for victory lay in negativism.

During his first two years out of office, Cleveland avoided conspicuous political activity. He did little more than maintain an extensive correspondence with politicians and keep his name before the public by making some speeches on nonexplosive subjects. His time was taken up largely with the pleasurable activities of a private citizen. These were the most enjoyable years of his life.

As a private citizen Cleveland practiced law, in association with the New York firm of Bangs, Stetson, Tracy,
and MacVeagh. This relationship came about through his
long friendship with Francis Lynde Stetson. Cleveland
found great satisfaction in this new role and in the financial speculation that he engaged in moderately on the
side. He did not bury himself in his work as of yore. At
his office he had time to chat at length with Stetson, an
attorney for such an important person as J. P. Morgan.

Cleveland's legal work was routine in nature. He served
chiefly as court referee, arbitrator and adviser. Although
his associates handled the important cases, Cleveland had
the unique experience of being the only ex-President to
argue before the Supreme Court. This was in October,
1890, when he participated in a minor case which concerned the financial liability of New Orleans in a drain-
age project. Oddly, the newspapers made no reference to
it; even more oddly, three of the four justices appointed
by Cleveland sat on the case. Two of these, Chief Justice
Fuller and Justice Lamar, were with the minority in
the five to three decision that went against Cleveland.

In summer the Clevelands lived simply in their cot-
tage, Gray Gables, at Buzzards Bay. There the considerable "fun" in Cleveland found expression in gay times
with neighbors and visitors; there he fished; and there
he played with daughter Ruth, who was born in 1891.
Later the Clevelands had three more children. In the
winter they led an active social life in New York, going
to parties given by the substantial folk and often attending plays on Broadway.

What Cleveland learned about events outside New York
and Buzzards Bay he acquired through his correspondence

and occasional confabs with Bourbon politicians and his conversations with the representatives and friends of the financial world among whom he moved. He read and traveled very little.

Meanwhile the tempo of life outside his little world was accelerating rapidly. Economic and political developments interested Cleveland and gradually drew him back into the thick of politics. It became increasingly apparent that the American public was paying a cruelly high price for the industrialization that was replacing agriculture as the dominant economic feature of the nation. The leaders of the industrial advance had not only successfully diverted a large share of the nation's capital and natural resources to their enterprises but had also accumulated additional capital by charging exorbitant prices for the goods and services they provided. The industrialists also, operating through investment bankers, had obtained capital from European sources and thereby incurred a heavy private national debt. The cost of carrying this indebtedness was passed on to the consumers.

The absence of either governmental or self-imposed restraints was dangerous to entrepreneurs as well as to those they victimized. Industrialization proceeded too fast and too far. The protests of workingmen and farmers mounted. Since 1887 the agricultural situation had deteriorated precipitously. Drought and low prices prevailed in the West and declining cotton prices in the South. In 1890 a brief but ominous financial panic and stock-market tumble resulted from the failure that year of Baring Brothers, a famous London bank engaged in financing American enterprises. The effect of this failure on the United States economy became increasingly serious after 1890. European creditors no longer accepted American securities to settle trade balances. They demanded gold, and though the United States Treasury still had a surplus, it was closer to a deficit than anybody could foresee.

The year 1890 was a busy one for the politicians. Congress enacted several important measures and then joined in a spirited mid-term election campaign. The Republican administration, its attention pragmatically focused on the political segments of the nation that promised greatest support, forged ahead with an aggressive legislative program.

The Republicans were counting on farm support in the ensuing election through their traditional hold on the Western farm vote, through the plausibility of the protective tariff argument and through a concession on the currency issue. The Republican response to the Treasury surplus seemed to the dogmatic Bourbons to reflect special privilege, demoralizing paternalism, and wasteful spending. The McKinley Act, "to equalize the duties upon imports and to reduce the revenues," raised the tariff on both farm and industrial products to a higher level than ever before. But tariff protection could not help the majority of farmers, whose problem was that of domestic rather than imported surpluses. Furthermore, higher duties on items purchased by the farmers added to their already-depressed condition. The McKinley Act attempted to reduce the surplus mainly through its provision to repeal the duty on raw sugar, one of the few agricultural commodities imported in large quantities and also produced in the United States. This provision was designed to please consumers in general, as well as to reduce the income from duties. Domestic sugar growers were granted a subsidy of two cents a pound. Sugar refiners, combined in a powerful Sugar Trust with a persuasive lobby to deal with politicians, were pleased with the levy of one half a cent a pound on refined sugar. Many farmers, bolstered by enemies of the Republicans, received the McKinley Act with hostility. They blamed the Act for much of the increasing spread between the low prices of the products they sold and the high prices of the items they purchased. Thus the tariff became a major issue in the 1890 election.

The Republican Congress acted with directness in solving the problem of the surplus inherited from the inflexible Cleveland administration. They spent it. This "billion-dollar Congress" found the Civil War veterans eager to cooperate. The Dependents' Pension Act raised the number of pensioners from 489,725 in 1889 to 966,012 in 1893 with a corresponding increase in cost from $89,000,000 to $157,000,000. The money spent for pensions, plus large sums appropriated for river and harbor improvements, federal buildings, coast defenses and such, quickly ended the surplus and actually caused concern about the threat of a deficit. Though in 1890 the surplus was $190,000,000, by January, 1893, it was reduced to $108,000,000 — not far from the supposed danger point of $100,000,000.

A promise to silverites in return for their votes on the McKinley Tariff led to enactment of the Sherman Silver Purchase Act. This measure required the Treasury to buy 4,500,000 ounces of silver each month at the market price, to pay for it in a new issue of notes and to store the silver in vaults as bullion. This measure proved less inflationary than its friends hoped and its enemies feared. For a brief time it absorbed most of the silver mined and hence kept the silver price up. But before 1892 increased production had substantially lowered the price of silver. The Treasury was thus able to purchase the required amount at a lower price, which meant the issuance of fewer Treasury notes to pay for the metal. Actually the Bland-Allison Act, which the Sherman Silver Purchase Act repealed, was preferable from the standpoint of the silver miners and inflationists. If in 1890 the Treasury had bought silver to the full amount of the $4,000,000 permitted (but never utilized) under the Bland-Allison Act, the amount of silver purchased when the price dropped would have increased and the inflation thereby would have been more marked.

Although the Sherman Silver Purchase Act came to displease silverites, it also angered many gold standard champions. The "goldbugs" felt that the law was a threat to the gold standard. The ever-increasing number of Treasury notes issued to purchase the silver bullion would have to be redeemable in gold at the Treasury if the nation were to maintain its gold currency base. The demand might become too great. Hence, the Republican Congress that passed the measure and President Harrison who signed it satisfied neither camp in the currency battle.

Cleveland was pleased with none of the Republican measures dealing with the tariff, currency and the surplus. But he held his peace publicly until after the 1890 election. It was unseemly for an ex-President to do otherwise.

The most important measure Congress enacted in 1890 was the Sherman Antitrust Act, which marked the federal government's initial commitment to destroy "combinations in restraint of trade" that could be interpreted as coming within the scope of the interstate commerce clause of the Constitution. But only in a negative sense did this law enter the Republican *vs.* Bourbon Democrat debate in the 1892 election campaign. In Congress it was debated and passed as a bipartisan measure, and most leaders in and out of Congress chose to keep it in that category. Business leaders and their political allies apparently decided that it was politically expedient to enact the measure as a concession to public demand and to avoid widespread public debate of the monopoly question in general, potentially an explosive subject. A bitter political battle on the subject might dislodge the dominant political friends of big business from their positions in both major parties. Indifference on the part of some leaders, coupled with the conviction that the Sherman Antitrust measure was innocuous, contributed both to its passage and to its failure to become a serious political issue. Cleveland was among those who ignored the Act, at least publicly.

During 1890, while Congress and the acquiescent President Harrison built up political storm fences in some places and pulled them down in others, a growing number of agrarian leaders were just as busily constructing an entirely new political alliance of their own. Already their feelings of desperation and of disgust with Republicans and Democrats alike had led them to abandon nonpartisan activity through the Farmers' Alliances and to make preparations for direct political action. In the Southern states, where Alliance men feared that the formation of independent party organizations might split the white vote and thereby permit Negro control, the agrarians attempted to capture the various state Democratic parties. That meant an effort to unseat the Redeemer element with whom Cleveland and Northern Bourbons were allied. In the Western states third parties sprang up, under such names as the People's party, the Independents, and the Independent Fusion. They entered the 1890 election campaign with astounding zeal and with a galaxy of remarkably gifted orators.

In this "pentecost of politics" the difference between the agrarian demands in the West and the South was chiefly in emphasis. In both cases farmers demanded action on currency and credit, railroad practices, public land disposal, the tariff, excessive landholding of railroads and alien land ownership. Convinced that men of wealth had deliberately manipulated the currency to decrease the supply, many urged enactment of the Subtreasury plan. This arresting proposal called for federal legislation to establish warehouses for the storage of nonperishable farm commodities, which in turn could serve as collateral for loans to the farmers who deposited their products. The farmers could obtain loans equal to eighty per cent of the market value of the stored commodities at one per cent interest. They would thereby benefit from the increased quantity of currency thus placed in circulation, for the loans would be in the form of newly issued notes based on the commodities in the warehouses. The system would add flexibility to the currency supply, for the notes would be issued when cash was most needed and then retired as processors and consumers emptied the warehouses and paid for their contents. In addition to government bonds, silver and gold, farm commodities would thus constitute a source of currency.

Not much in the talk of the agrarian agitators of 1890 appealed to Cleveland, except what was said about the high

tariff ogre. It was doubtful if he read the speeches of Ignatius Donnelly, Jerry Simpson, Thomas Watson, Mary Eliza-
beth Lease and other earnest rebels against the *status
quo*. While Cleveland was in his Broad Street office, Mrs.
Lease was telling a Kansas audience something about Wall
Street. The attractive, thirty-seven-year-old Irish-American Mrs. Lease said that "Wall Street owns the country. . . . The great common people of this country are
slaves, and monopoly is the master. The West and South
are bound and prostrate before the manufacturing
East. . . . The parties lie to us and the political speak-
ers mislead us. . . . The politicians said we suffered from
overproduction. Overproduction when 10,000 little children, so statistics tell us, starve to death every year in the
United States, and over 100,000 shop-girls in New York
are forced to sell their virtue for the bread their nig-
gardly wages deny them. . . . Kansas suffers from two
great robbers, the Santa Fe Railroad and the loan companies. . . . We want money, land and transportation.
We want the abolition of the National Banks, and we want
the power to make loans direct from the government."
Such were the outbursts in the political sideshows of the
1890 campaign.

The 1890 campaign was intensely spirited—especially
in the depressed agrarian areas. On the national front
the Republicans presented a crowded two-year record for
review, and the Democrats eagerly went forth to inform
the voters to judge it. The Democrats drew voter attention to the unimpressive Republican record on civil service, the wasteful pork-barrel legislation, the Dependents' Pension Act, the tyranny of Speaker of the House
"Czar" Thomas B. Reed, the efforts to revive North-South

sectionalism by clamoring for the Force bill, which would impose federal control of elections in the South, and the McKinley Tariff. Inflationists in all the parties talked much of free silver, while the goldbugs attempted to dodge the issue. Of all the national issues the tariff received by far the greatest attention and contributed most to the election outcome. Some areas witnessed equally heated debate over state issues. Nativists and "foreigners," puritans and nonpuritans engaged in bitter fighting over the liquor and parochial school issues.

In 1890 and at other times during the post-Civil War era, these social cleavages were often as much responsible for the election outcome in some states as were national economic questions, or more. For example, in the 1889 Iowa election, prohibition was an important factor in refuting Congressman Jonathan P. Dolliver's prediction that Iowa "would go Democratic when hell went Methodist." In 1890 the same issue was influential in Nebraska, Minnesota and several other states; in 1890 and 1892 the parochial school question perhaps changed more votes in Wisconsin and Illinois than did any other issue. But the greatest single, underlying influence on the outcome was the general discontent resulting from the hard times. In New England, manufacturing was sluggish; in the agricultural West and South, such prices prevailed as six-cent cotton, fifteen-cent oats, and thirty-cent corn, with interest rates ten per cent and more.

The outcome was an astoundingly large number of Democrats elected, a surprisingly large number of agrarian insurgents elected, and the most emphatic defeat for the Republicans since the party was born. The sweep carried into the House 235 Democrats and 9 independent, third-party agrarians and eliminated all but 88 Republicans. In the Senate, the Republican majority was reduced to 8. The greatest Republican reversals were in the agrarian West, but added to them were also such setbacks as the loss of the governorship in Massachusetts to Democratic tariff reformer William E. Russell. In the over-all result there were two especially important facts — the obvious one that the prospects for Democratic victory in the 1892 presidential election were bright, and the less conspicuous one that a determined agrarian political revolt had begun.

Cleveland, elated over the election outcome, assumed a definitely receptive attitude toward the sentiment that he become his party's 1892 standard-bearer. The tone and quantity of his letter writing and speeches bespoke a desire to return to the White House. In the spirited contest for the Democratic nomination Cleveland's greatest asset was his popularity with the voters, which would inevitably influence delegates to the nominating convention. The public tended to make comparisons between him and the incumbent President, and there was a strong current of public longing for the return of Cleveland. The admirers and advocates of "good government" saw Cleveland as a bulwark against hordes of unworthy office seekers and pension grabbers and bad practices in administrative departments. In the record of the colorless Harrison, whatever was good in this respect was overshadowed by his signature on such measures as the Dependents' Pension Act. Economy-minded citizens saw Cleveland as a watchful guardian over the public till, and Harrison as a man who had allowed the surplus in the Treasury to be dissipated by both the "pension steal" and a host of pork-barrel appropriations. Worshipers of the gold standard saw Cleveland as a Gibraltar of strength against the irresponsible silverites, whereas Harrison had signed into law the reprehensible Sherman Silver Purchase sop. Devotees of tariff reform recalled Cleveland's 1887 outburst and shuddered at Harrison's acceptance of the McKinley Tariff.

These citizens and many others were moved by a feeling of need for protection by a wise, reliable and brave public father. Their economic security was threatened by a creeping depression and by a revengeful rabble elbowing its way into the seats of power. Harrison was a man without resolution. Cleveland might lack the necessary qualities for bringing about a legislative program of reform, but at least he had proved himself capable of standing firmly against evil.

Cleveland possessed another asset in his association with the Bourbon element of the Democracy. He had forged strong ties with many members of that group and could count on the loyalty of such strong political figures as former Cabinet officer Vilas, who controlled the Democracy in Wisconsin and was elected in 1891 to the Senate. In Minnesota the powerful Jim Hill-Mike Doran-Pat Kelly triumvirate added its strength. Governor Russell of Massachusetts, Don M. Dickinson of Michigan, Congressman Wilson of West Virginia and Whitney of New York were among very loyal and influential Cleveland supporters.

In 1890, however, a major obstruction stood in the road to renomination. An ominously large number of party leaders were outside the Cleveland camp. The discontent apparent in the 1888 campaign had increased. The party organization in vitally important New York State was definitely controlled by anti-Cleveland politicians, and in the South and West the increased popularity of the currency inflation advocates had produced a corresponding antagonism toward goldbug Cleveland. His popularity among voters and Bourbons was too widely dispersed, too thin in the states where it was crucially important. It had been that way in 1888; it had become more so since 1888.

The New York State situation was the chief obstacle. Governor Hill controlled the state organization and was an aggressive contender for the presidential nomination. Many Democratic politicians, anxious to check Cleveland, contended that New York in 1892 would go to the Democratic party with Hill as the candidate but not with Cleveland. The 1888 election results had shown emphatically that Hill was popular and Cleveland was not. And since then the shrewd and ambitious Hill and his state-wide machine had worked diligently to widen the gap, assuming that "nothing succeeds like success."

Hill's success at the 1892 convention might well prove a fatal blow to the Bourbon Democracy. The basic factor in Hill's political strength was his emphasis on machine tactics, on appeals to emotional loyalty to the party label, and on concessions to popular opinion and pressure groups even when they violated sound economic, social and governmental dogmas. The Cleveland-Bourbon group relied more on the Democratic voters' fixed devotion to conservative and traditional ideas and on an appeal to voters inside and outside the party fold who placed devotion to honest and efficient government above loyalty to party organizations. As of 1890 it was not inevitable that the relatively inflexible, theoretical Bourbon approach was equal to obtaining control of the 1892 convention. Cleveland was well aware of Hill's strength and intentions. On November 8, just after the 1890 election, Cleveland wrote to Bissell: "Of one thing you may be entirely certain. Hill and his friends are bent on his nomination for the Presidency, and failing in that they are determined that it shall not come toward me."

The anti-Cleveland sentiment among Southern and Western Democrats was noisy but too uncrystallized to measure in terms of future delegate votes. The 1890 election results nevertheless showed that the old bugaboo of a West-South agrarian alliance to replace the East-South Bourbon alliance had made its appearance with greater than usual force. Agrarian leaders and silver mine operators were converging behind the free-silver banner. It was conceivable that the result would be the isolation and defeat of Cleveland and all Bourbons if they remained uncompromising on the currency issue.

With the stage thus set in 1890, Cleveland and Hill began to bid with mounting intensity for the leading role. Some lesser lights moved about quietly among fellow politicians and citizens, receptive to suggestions that they be on hand in case Cleveland and Hill became politically indisposed. The wily Senator Gorman of Maryland was one of the ablest political manipulators of the era. Not far distant was a newcomer, Governor Horace Boies of Iowa, "with a Mona Lisa smile on his affidavit face," who had proved that a Democrat could get elected in rock-ribbed Republican Iowa. But none of these hopefuls managed to get very close to the center of the stage.

The free-silver issue was the most important item influencing the outcome of the preconvention contest for the nomination. In January, 1891, the Senate passed, although the House later rejected, a free coinage of silver bill. Democratic Senators and free-silver Republicans had joined forces to bring it about. The only Democrat to vote in the negative was George Gray of Delaware. This did not mean that all the other Democratic Senators actually favored the measure. They were rather partners in a deal. This was the price they paid to the free-silver Republicans to defeat the Lodge Federal Elections Force bill, designed to insure Negro voting in the South. This Democratic action was nevertheless a blow to the Cleveland Bourbons. It not only gave impetus to the silverite crusade but was evidence that the Democratic Senators were unwilling or felt unable to resist pressure that carried them far afield from the firm, traditional Bourbon stand on currency.

The free-silver issue contained ingredients that in an environment of severe economic hardship might carry its advocates to supreme power. As more and more citizens reached the point of desperation, they grasped at straws. They were attracted to cure-all schemes and most especially to those that seemed to promise quick financial relief. "Good government" and tariff reform had appealed to many citizens as cure-alls, but neither of those supposed panaceas offered the quick, extensive results envisioned in a flow of money spilling forth from the silver-fed machines. Advocates of free silver were well supplied with arguments. In answer to the doctrinaire gold standard contention that the law of supply and demand would cause an increase in gold production as the need arose, they pointed out that the per capita supply of money was declining and thereby causing the price level to decline. Silverites also argued that free coinage would result in a stable price level, because the market price of silver was following the same general curve as other products.

Gold standard advocates, persuaded by Gresham's law that cheap money would drive expensive money out of circulation, feared lest the United States lose its gold as silver poured in from other nations. Owners of foreign silver could sell it for gold in America at the profitable official rate of 16 to 1. This process would soon leave the United States without gold to meet foreign obligations. Antisilverites also envisaged a continuous flow of foreign silver into the country large enough to cause disastrous inflation.

The silverites contended, however, that government purchases of silver would absorb enough to enhance its price on the world market and thereby prevent its concentration at home. In any case the silverites were not averse to deflating foreign, especially British, pocketbooks and inflating domestic prices. Which arguments were the more valid could be discovered only by giving free silver a trial.

The free silverites possessed an important political asset, in addition to the attraction their panacea offered indebted farmers and profit-seeking silver miners. They had taken the offensive. Hard times called for action, and the gold standard leaders were without a positive program. An increasing number of hard money men, most notably in the banking community, admitted the need for more currency, but they failed to agree upon a means to achieve that end. Various compromise plans and alternatives floated around, but not one of them attracted powerful or sustained political sponsorship. The most popular proposal, aside from the agrarian Subtreasury plan, was international bimetallism — whereby both gold and silver currency would be used throughout the world, with the ratio between both metals fixed artificially by international agreement. This would prevent the operation of Gresham's law, for both currencies would be guaranteed equality in purchasing power.

Important antifree-silver national political leaders dismissed international bimetallism and other plans as unfeasible and adopted instead a defensive position. They appealed for popular support, using the familiar devices of ridicule, empty promises for reform and attempts to instill fear of change, and they employed political discipline on party underlings. Cleveland used this approach — after it became politically necessary for him to become closely involved in the currency question.

The Senate vote for free silver, in January, 1891, plus the fact that newspapers had been circulating the rumor that Cleveland had become converted to free silver, aroused the ex-President to a state of fury. Ever since he was rebuffed by the House Democrats early in his Presidency and especially from the time he chose tariff reform as the most important economic goal, Cleveland had avoided direct involvement in the currency issue. He had not changed his views on free silver but had simply become more politically expedient. This cautious avoidance of the topic gave plausibility to the rumor that he had reversed his former conservative opposition. More important, the rumor and the growth of free-silver sentiment forced Cleveland into an awkward position. Silence would aid the despised politicians bent on making free silver the central issue in the 1892 campaign. He believed that the tariff was both the most important issue and the one best calculated to advance his and the Democratic party's fortunes. Cleveland also believed, as he revealed to Don Dickinson, that the noise over silver was a Republican trick to becloud the tariff issue.

Cleveland conferred with some of his associates on how to handle the matter. The loyal Whitney, who was soon to become director of the Bourbon cabal working for Cleveland's nomination, advocated silence, as he had in 1887 on the tariff issue. But the others in the group did not share Whitney's nervousness. Hence, with the blessing and aid of his onetime Secretary of Treasury Fairchild, his former private secretary and close adviser Lamont, New York railroad lawyer Ellery E. Anderson and a few other allies, Cleveland prepared for action.

With the decision made, it was arranged that Anderson, on behalf of the Reform Club, invite Cleveland to a dinner meeting to express New York businessmen's opposition to free silver. Cleveland answered this invitation in a letter dated February 10, 1891, and released to the press. The final letter, shortened markedly as it went through the processes of several drafts, expressed Cleveland's regrets at not being able to attend and made two key points bearing on his silver currency views. Both points were included in the one pertinent sentence of the letter: "If we have developed an unexpected capacity for the assimilation of a largely increased volume of this currency, and even if we have demonstrated the usefulness of such an increase, these conditions fall far short of insuring us against disaster if, in the present situation, we enter upon the dangerous and reckless experiment of free, unlimited, and independent silver coinage."

It was a cleverly devised statement. In effect Cleveland branded the silverites as being irresponsible and hence to be shunned by sober-minded, intelligent citizens. Coming from a widely respected leader, this blunt outburst certainly could cause many confused, ill-informed and fence-sitting citizens to hesitate to join the silverite "mob." At the same time, Cleveland's other point implied that he was not adamantly opposed to a controlled silver coinage program. While in the mid-1880's he had called emphatically for repeal of the silver purchase feature of the Bland-Allison Act, he now did not even suggest repeal of the Sherman Silver Purchase Act of 1890. His opposition to "independent silver coinage" could be interpreted as a hint that he might accept silver coinage through international agreement. Reactionaries might have been a little disappointed in Cleveland's bow to political expediency, but they could find comfort in his blast at free silver and in the use of the word "if" to indicate his lack of certainty that increased use of silver was wise.

The letter had the desired effect. A flood of friendly political comment came forth from both moderate bimetallists and goldbugs. The letter also served as a useful reminder to citizens and politicians that Cleveland was still around.

Cleveland delivered several speeches during the ensuing months that helped keep his name before the public. In October, 1891, in an address before the Business Men's Democratic Association in Madison Square Garden, Cleveland appealed to businessmen to be more active in politics and, incidentally, to support the New York State Democratic ticket of that fall. "It must be confessed," he said, "that . . . those engaged in business pursuits have kept too much aloof from public affairs. . . .

I am firmly of the belief that, if a few business men could be substituted for professional men in official places, the people would positively gain by the exchange."

On January 8, 1892, when that same association met to celebrate the anniversary of Andrew Jackson's victory at New Orleans, Cleveland was again the speaker. Always a great admirer of Jackson, Cleveland used the occasion to evoke the spirit of that great leader for the present day. He reviewed Jackson's attack on the United States Bank, stating that he fought it "utterly regardless of any considerations of political expediency or personal advancement. . . ." Jackson "allowed nothing to divert him from his complete triumph . . . and permitted no other issue to divide his energy or be substituted for that on which he was intent." Then Cleveland turned to the present. "We have insisted on tariff reform and on abandonment of unjust favoritism. We have thus adopted an issue great enough to deserve the undivided efforts of our party." Thereby, without direct reference to free silver, Cleveland sought to bury that subject and to keep tariff reform the central aim of the party. "If," he concluded, "inspired by the true Jacksonian spirit, we hold to the doctrine that party honesty is party duty and party courage is party expediency, we shall win a sure and lasting success through the deserved support of a discriminating, intelligent, and thoughtful people."

Cleveland was now aided by the errors of Hill, by the growing fear among conservatives and moderates that free silver was a danger to their property, and by the skillful political activity of Whitney and other loyal Bourbons.

Though, during 1891, Hill was widely considered a likely recipient of the nomination, he was at the same time sowing seeds of dissatisfaction that might well produce defeat. In January, 1891, he used his power over the legislature to obtain his own election to the United States Senate after having earlier indicated that he would back Smith W. Weed for the job. Hill's reversal angered Weed's numerous friends and irritated several influential members of Hill's own state machine. Then Hill, fearing he would lose control of his machine if he resigned the governorship upon his election to the Senate, decided to retain both positions until the Senate convened ten months later. That extraordinary decision caused many to question the wisdom of making Hill President. Late in 1891 he began to show too much friendship toward free silver to suit conservatives. Hill emphasized his disapproval of the Sherman Silver Purchase Act and his approval of bimetallism, but simply did not reveal whether or not he favored a bimetallic system that included unrestricted coinage of silver. Tariff reformers were unenthusiastic over Hill's views. Though he asked for repeal of the McKinley Tariff, he would then return the nation to the still-high 1883 schedules. In so doing he was bidding for the support of such protectionists as Gorman of Maryland and Brice of Ohio, who were anxious to prevent Cleveland's nomination. All these items were filed away in the memories of citizens to be used in 1892.

While Cleveland and Hill sparred with each other, farmers in the West and South became more discontented with their economic plight and hence became more active politically, a situation which in turn tended to sober conservatives and moderates and caused them to turn away from the untrustworthy Hill toward the reliable Cleveland. It also stepped up the political activity of conservatives. Some rich Republicans, distrustful of Harrison because of his signature on the Sherman Silver Purchase Act, turned to Cleveland. Wealthy railroader and banker Henry Villard was among them. An 1891 tour of his Northern Pacific Railroad showed him conditions that convinced him that a depression was on the way and a dangerous political situation was brewing. He saw agrarian legislators spreading "an epidemic of dishonesty . . . manifesting itself in the most outrageous legislative violence to railroads and the free coinage of silver infatuation." In 1891, and especially in 1892, Villard extensively used his powers of persuasion and his substantial bank account for Cleveland.

During early 1892 the Cleveland candidacy gained momentum, and by May it was practically certain that he would win at the convention, on June 21. Hill supporters in New York contributed to this pro-Cleveland drift. The New York state Democratic commitee, controlled by chairman Edward Murphy and other Hill men, set February 22 as the date for the state convention to elect four delegates at large to the national convention. Normally it met in late April. This earlier date was chosen with the expectation that snowbound roads might prevent anti-Hill Democrats in upstate rural regions from attending local caucuses that selected delegates to the state meeting. Decent citizens in New York State and elsewhere were infuriated at this highhanded trick. It was all that was needed to bring down the already close-to-the-ground Hill kite.

Early in March, 1892, Cleveland wrote a letter for publication, and announced his willingness to be President again. Once more, as in his statement on silver a year earlier, he employed the "if" device. He modestly told Bragg that "if you are right in supposing that the subject is related to a duty I owe to the country and to my party, a condition exists which makes . . . private and personal considerations entirely irrelevant." Then, after remarking on the burdensome nature of the Presidency and the "solemnity of the trust," Cleveland made clear he was not going to campaign actively for it. He said: "I cannot bring myself to regard a candidacy for the place as something to be won by personal strife and active self-assertion."

Whitney headed the Cleveland forces. An associate in the work, George F. Parker, later described Whitney as particularly well fitted for the task. "Generally indifferent to details . . . he had the rare gift of doing within a few days the work that would require weeks on the part of the average leader." Whitney applied his "marvelous power of concentration, amounting almost to genius," to the work. He drew upon his own enormous bank account and inspired other rich men to contribute generously. He jogged Cleveland into making an active bid for delegates, through letters to politicians and a trip to Rhode Island. Whitney shrewdly reduced the anti-Cleveland attitude among New York politicians, even wringing a promise from boss Richard Croker that Tammany would not oppose Cleveland in the fall election.

On June 9, to make secret preparations for the June 21 opening day of the convention, Whitney gathered a conference at his residence, notice of which was kept from outsiders. In 1909, Parker wrote: "From that day to this I have never seen any notice of its existence — to say nothing of its proceedings." Among those present were

Don M. Dickinson, William F. Vilas, William L. Wilson, John E. Russell, Josiah Quincy, Francis Lynde Stetson, William F. Harrity and George F. Parker. The conferees selected their men for membership on the important convention committees and made arrangements for recruiting more Bourbons to meet with them occasionally at the convention. Doubtless they also discussed the platform to be adopted at the convention. Vilas was selected as the person to get the conferees' views written into the platform. He was to be chairman of the Committee on Resolutions. He was a foe of free silver, a longtime advocate of tariff reform, a loyal and close friend of Cleveland's and a newly elected Senator with great influence among Middle Western Bourbons.

At the convention the major items in the plans of the Cleveland group were carried out, with one exception. The exception was a failure to obtain majority delegate support for the tariff plank proposed by the Committee on Resolutions. The proposed platform showed clearly that Bourbon strategy was to concentrate Democratic fire on the Republican record and to offer in its place simply a return to the "good old days."

The resolution on the tariff, which proved to be unacceptable to the majority of the convention delegates, was an emotional attack on the McKinley Tariff, followed by a completely negative substitute proposal. The resolution would simply have the tariff duties returned to the pre-McKinley schedules. It termed the McKinley Tariff "the culminating atrocity of class legislation," and then called for a judicious revision that would not injure "any domestic industries." Tariff reformer Vilas and the other Bourbons seemingly wished it forgotten that they had supported Cleveland's 1887 tariff message and the Mills bill. But a minority on the committee, led by editor "Marse" Henry Watterson and Congressman Tom L. Johnson, carried the fight for reform to the floor of the convention. They succeeded in getting a substitute resolution passed that not only denounced "Republican protection as a fraud, a robbery of the great majority of the American people for the benefit of the few," but also reiterated the often-neglected but traditional Democratic party principle "that the Federal government has no constitutional power to collect tariff duties except for the purpose of revenue only. . . ." It was a free trade plank.

On the silver question the proposed resolution, which was accepted by the convention, hit hard at the Republican-sponsored Sherman Silver Purchase Act, characterizing it as a "cowardly makeshift." This attack on a specific Republican measure was accompanied by a vague statement of a possible alternative: "We hold to the use of both gold and silver as the standard money of the country, and to the coinage of both gold and silver, without discriminating against either metal. . . ." The door was left open for legislation or international agreement that conceivably could provide for extensive silver coinage. It was not clear whether these Democrats favored more or less silver coinage than was provided by the Sherman Silver Purchase Act. But they clearly wanted a more stable currency, for they stated at the end of the resolution: "We insist upon this policy as especially necessary for the protection of the farmers and laboring classes, the first and most defenseless victims of unstable money and a fluctuating currency."

It was apparent from the outset that Cleveland would

win the nomination. The only possible threat, that of the Gorman backers, collapsed before it was organized. Gorman recognized that he could not possibly defeat Cleveland, so he discouraged the movement on his behalf. Cleveland was nominated on the first ballot.

The vice-presidential nomination went to Adlai Stevenson of Illinois. He was a professional politician in the sense that he understood and practiced politics in accordance with the traditional rules of the game. As Assistant Postmaster General in Cleveland's administration, he had conscientiously and efficiently worked with Congressmen and other politicians on patronage disposal. Stevenson rooted his political strength in the agrarian environment of Illinois, rather than in the Eastern Bourbonism of Cleveland. He accepted the idea of free silver. In acceding to his candidacy for the Vice-Presidency, the Bourbons were giving the silverites a sop and they were also hoping as a result that Illinois might go Democratic. The Bourbons apparently reasoned that Cleveland's rugged health was insurance against a silverite Vice-President's becoming President. This proved to be a greater gamble than they anticipated, for Cleveland's health went through a crisis that might well have proved fatal.

The election campaign that followed and the outcome were basically repetitious of 1890, but projected onto the broader national scale. Republicans still had to carry the burdensome defense of their unpopular legislative record, with the addition now of a plea for the return to office of the uninspiring Harrison. To nominate someone else would be admission of a mistake, so they dutifully renominated Harrison and defended the record of his administration.

The agrarians, extending their political protest of 1890, organized the People's, or Populist, party. They launched the party in May, 1891, and then in June, 1892, they held a national nominating convention. The Populist platform emphasized land, transportation and finance as the principal issues. It called for an increase in the currency by a direct issuance of paper money, or by the "free and unlimited coinage of silver at the ratio of sixteen to one," or by both means. It urged government ownership and operation of the railroads and the telegraph and telephone systems; and the return to the government of lands granted to "railroads and other corporations" that were in "excess of their actual needs." It condemned alien land ownership and endorsed the Subtreasury plan; the Australian ballot; a graduated income tax; postal savings banks; shorter hours for labor; direct election of United States Senators; the initiative, referendum and recall; and a single term for the President and Vice-President. Their nominee was James B. Weaver of Iowa, who in 1880 had been the Greenback candidate.

Cleveland reacted to the course of events with more interest than he had shown in the 1884 and 1888 contests. That he was clearly intent upon victory was made apparent through the numerous letters he wrote to politicians, the very politic appeal for votes in his acceptance address and the conciliatory attitude he finally adopted in order to win the support of powerful New York Democrats whom he personally despised.

In preparing his acceptance address, Cleveland devoted particular attention to the tariff issue, which, he informed Charles S. Hamlin, gave him "some perplexity." He worried over how to deal with the free trade plank in the platform. On July 9 he wrote to Whitney: "Ever since I read the plank in the platform . . . I have been very much annoyed and fearful about it. I am irritated too because I can plainly see the thing was started in malice and carried out in malignity." He placed the blame chiefly on Tammany but also had something to say about "this fellow Watterson." Cleveland felt that "the sooner he is given his place on the furtherest back seat the safer we shall be." But he was in a quandary over where to place the tariff plank. "I think," he suggested to Whitney, "I must stand by the message of 1887 and if I make up my mind to that, I shall come pretty near saying so."

On that same day Watterson wrote to Cleveland in a manner that showed he entertained no doubts on what course to pursue: "You cannot escape your great message of 1887 if you would. Take it as your guiding star. Stand up to it. Reiterate it. Emphasize it, amplify it, but do not subtract a thought, do not erase a word. . . ." Watterson clearly felt that Cleveland needed to be nudged in such fashion to counteract pressure from the opposite side. He included in his letter: "If you will allow me to say so, in perfect frankness and without intending to be rude or unkind, the gentlemen immediately about you, gentlemen upon whom you rely for material and energetic party management, are not, as to the tariff, Democrats at all; and have little conception of the place in the popular mind and heart held by the Revenue Reform idea, or indeed of any idea, except that of organization and money. . . ." Cleveland, greatly irritated, included in his testy reply to Watterson the observation: "If we are defeated this year, I predict a Democratic wandering in the dark wilds of discouragement for twenty-five years. I do not propose to be at all responsible for such a result."

The statement on the tariff in his acceptance address showed that Cleveland had decided that to "stand by the message of 1887" might result in Democratic "wandering in the dark wilds." He began with a statement that obviously was designed to please the doctrinaire advocates of "tariff for revenue only," i.e., free trade. He described the tariff as a form of taxation, "representing a diminution of the property rights of the people," and justifiable only "when laid and collected for the purpose of maintaining our Government and furnishing the means for the accomplishment of its legitimate purposes and functions." But it turned out that Cleveland considered protective duties one of these "legitimate purposes and functions." He stated that "we wage no exterminating war against any American interests. We believe a readjustment can be accomplished in accordance with the principles we profess without disaster or demolition." In short, he said, we favor "a fair and careful distribution of necessary tariff burdens rather than the precipitation of free trade."

In his acceptance address Cleveland showed as much caution on the silver question as on the tariff: "The people are entitled to sound and honest money abundantly sufficient in volume to supply their business needs." He hinted opposition to free silver and open-mindedness on alternative proposals, by adding that "whatever may be the form of the people's currency, national or State — whether gold, silver or paper — it should be so regulated and guarded by governmental action or by wise and careful laws that no one can be deluded as to the certainty and stability of its value."

In the course of the campaign Cleveland made a friendly gesture toward influential New York politicians. As with most actions of Cleveland during the campaign, Whitney supplied the inspiration. But in this instance Whitney had great difficulty persuading Cleveland to bury his animosity against the New Yorkers who had supported Hill. Whitney was convinced that if Cleveland showed a conciliatory attitude toward state committee chairman Edward Murphy, Tammany boss Croker and boss William F. Sheehan of Buffalo, they would actively support the campaign in New York and thereby insure a Democratic victory in that state. Otherwise New York, and hence the national election, would almost certainly go to Harrison. Cleveland exploded wrathfully when Whitney suggested that he send a friendly letter to Murphy. "I'll see the whole outfit to the devil before I'll do it," he told Bissell. His refusal enraged Whitney and caused him to tell Cleveland: "If you think best not to even write a friendly letter to the Chairman of your State Committee who has come in and is acting in your interest to straighten out difficulties, I had better stop where I am." In the end, Cleveland agreed to meet with Murphy, Sheehan and Croker to talk matters over. At the meeting the political trio and Cleveland agreed to work harmoniously in order to carry the state. Whitney later helped matters, according to Croker, through such gestures as the inclusion of the Tammany boss in a betting pool that Whitney organized to change the odds from Harrison's to Cleveland's favor. Whitney used his own money to put Croker in for $100,000, and after the election handed $100,000 to Croker as his share of the profit of the pool. Whitney had wanted the influential Croker's name in the pool.

An important reason for Cleveland's hesitancy to swallow his pride and to approach these New York leaders was his belief, for a time, that he could win the Presidency without the New York vote. He was hopeful of carrying enough states in the Middle West to offset the loss of New York. It appeared that Illinois and Wisconsin would repeat their 1890 performance by going Democratic. In Illinois John Peter Altgeld was carrying on an impressive campaign for the governorship; in Wisconsin, work done by the efficient organization headed by Vilas and managed by astute Edward C. Wall of Milwaukee was equally impressive. In both states the parochial school question, kept alive in part through the financial contributions of Henry Villard, gave promise of Democratic converts from the ranks of the many Catholics and Lutherans. Whitney was less optimistic than Cleveland about prospects in Illinois and Wisconsin and insisted on following the usual Bourbon practice of virtually ignoring the Middle West. He persuaded Cleveland to do likewise. As it turned out, those two states went Democratic.

The outcome of the election was a decisive victory for Cleveland and his party. The score for Cleveland was 5,556,000; Harrison, 5,175,000; Weaver, 1,041,000. The Democrats obtained a majority in both Houses, and the Populists won ten seats in the House and five in the Senate. For the third time Cleveland had obtained a majority popular vote over a Republican presidential candidate, and each time by a substantially wider margin. Republican prestige was at a low point; the Populists had failed to hurt the Democratic party. The result might well afford Cleveland and the Democracy great confidence.

VIII
Depression Legislation

THROUGHOUT the second Cleveland administration a fearsome economic depression buffeted the nation. Economic insecurity strained men's emotional stability. In larger numbers than usual people turned to the national government for relief, assurance or protection. They looked in particular to President Cleveland. As chief executive and as head of the party that controlled Congress, he alone was in a position to lead the nation to safety. He was known to have integrity and courage, and he could be counted on to do what he deemed to be safe and sound.

What Cleveland did do during those critical years gratified many people and angered many others. In 1897, Republican Senator Allison of Iowa was to reflect: "It was God's mercy to this country that Grover Cleveland, and not Harrison, was elected President." But in 1895 Democratic Governor John Peter Altgeld of Illinois stated: "To laud Clevelandism on Jefferson's birthday is to sing a Te Deum in honor of Judas Iscariot on a Christmas morning!"

The depression was still in its preliminary stage during the period between the election and the time Cleveland took office. The economic structure was wobbly enough to cause widespread concern about the future, but it did not collapse and precipitate public panic until a few weeks after his inauguration. Until then Cleveland concentrated on choosing his Cabinet and on deciding how best to attack the grave financial situation draining the Treasury of its gold reserve.

The Cabinet Cleveland selected was tinged with Bourbonism, although this was less apparent at the outset than after it began to function. Secretary of State Walter Q. Gresham was not a Bourbon, but neither did he wield influence outside his State Department duties. Gresham was a high-minded, deeply intelligent, liberal Republican who had demonstrated Populist leanings. He had left the G.O.P. during the 1892 campaign and cast his vote for Cleveland. His appointment, which came as a surprise to everybody, was made after Bayard and apparently several others had refused the position. Secretary of the Treasury John G. Carlisle had demonstrated definite silverite leanings, but he nevertheless became very useful to the Bourbon cause. Being pliable and at the same time intelligent and likable, Carlisle labored effectively among his former colleagues in Congress to obtain support for Bourbon financial policies. To Benjamin R. Tillman, South Carolina agrarian leader, Carlisle was "the Judas from Kentucky."

The other members of the Cabinet had professional records or personal ties with Cleveland that insured their loyalty to Bourbonism. Postmaster General Bissell was Cleveland's law partner of Buffalo days. Secretary of War

Lamont became the "assistant president," which in a less pronounced way had been his role when he was private secretary during Cleveland's previous administration. Upon leaving the White House in 1889 he had fallen in with important businessmen in New York and soon acquired considerable money through stock-market speculation. Appointed to the Cabinet at the suggestion of Whitney, who refused a post for himself, Lamont proved to be both an intimate adviser to Cleveland and the chief liaison officer between New York Bourbons and the White House. Attorney General Richard S. Olney, who became Secretary of State after the death of Gresham in 1895 and was a newcomer to the world of politics, was a bulwark of Bourbonism. He had been known only as an able and conservative Boston corporation lawyer, but he had strong New York support for a Cabinet position. Cleveland unwisely came to place great reliance on him.

Secretary of Agriculture J. Sterling Morton, the father of Arbor Day, was known for his zealous dedication to free trade, his assiduous lobbying for railroad corporations and his leadership of the Nebraska Bourbons. Shortly after entering the Cabinet, he delivered an address at the Chicago World's Fair that left farmers no doubt as to his economic views. "The most insidious and destructive foe to the farmer," said Morton, "is the 'professional' farmer who, as a 'promoter' of granges and alliances, for political purposes, *Farms the Farmer*. . . ." He recommended the study of Adam Smith's *The Wealth of Nations,* which was "to political economy as the New Testament is to the Christian religion." For supplementary reading the farmers should read each day in a newspaper "from a great city" that fought for free trade and no restrictions upon private accumulation of wealth. The editors of the *Forum* and the *North American Review* were impressed enough by this performance to induce Morton to write articles in the same vein for their periodicals.

In addition to Carlisle, there were two Southerners on the Cabinet. When appointed, Secretary of the Interior Hoke Smith was unknown outside his region. Lamar urged the selection of this Georgian, and Smith himself had gone to great lengths to inform Cleveland of his successful efforts to defeat the supporters of Hill in Georgia. The New York *Sun* named him "Hoax Myth." Secretary of the Navy Hilary A. Herbert was an ultra-Bourbon from Alabama. He had edited *Why the Solid South,* the most influential apology for the Southern Redeemer upsurge. Clearly this element of the South was as well represented as when Lamar and Garland served on the previous Cleveland Cabinet. Soon too, after the death of Lamar, Cleveland appointed a Louisiana Bourbon, Senator Edward D. White, to the Supreme Court. White was president of a large sugar refinery and a wealthy planter.

As Cleveland gave attention to the national economic situation, two related economic problems loomed large. One was the distress of many citizens and the general instability of the national economic-financial structure. The other was the precarious condition of the government's currency system. To Cleveland the problem was not one of finding new remedies but of deciding which remedy should be administered at which time. He believed that the major causes of the economic difficulties of both the citizens and the government were the Sher-

man Silver Purchase Act (which he ignored during the
election campaign) and the McKinley Tariff. Whatever
else was wrong in the national economy was due to the
folly or misfortune of individuals, and hence outside the
jurisdiction of the federal government. Local communi-
ties could attend to whatever human suffering existed in
their midst.

With his responsibility thus narrowed, Cleveland gradually decided to concentrate his initial effort on repeal of
the Silver Purchase Act. The pressure of events in the
financial world and the pressure exerted on him by finan-
ciers led him in that direction. In January, 1893, the
gold reserve was so low that the Harrison administration
had been forced to borrow $6,000,000 in gold from New
York banks in order to prevent the surplus from going
below $100,000,000. Silver and paper currency never-
theless continued to appear at the Treasury to be re-
deemed in gold. When Cleveland assumed office, the
reserve was only $100,982,410.

Meanwhile, many business leaders, with Lamont and
Don Dickinson often acting as their emissaries, made
known to Cleveland their belief that it was important for
him to call an extra session of Congress as soon as possible
to repeal the Sherman Silver Purchase Act. Henry Villard
was especially insistent on this move. Shortly before Inauguration Day, Cleveland permitted Villard to meet
with the Cabinet to present his point of view. A large
number of business leaders who favored repeal nevertheless advocated enactment of a substitute measure that
would provide for currency expansion and flexibility.
Their reasons varied from honest convictions to the belief
that Congress would not accept repeal without concessions

to the inflationists. Jacob Schiff, of Kuhn, Loeb & Company, favored action, but in the form of a compromise measure to placate silverites. J. P. Morgan also favored a temporary compromise measure, until the financial crisis ended. Andrew Carnegie, as late as April, 1893, believed "confidence" would return if Cleveland simply announced: "As long as I am President of the United States, the workingman is going to be paid in as good a dollar as the banker is." In May, Henry L. Higginson, of Lee, Higginson and Company, Boston, said that Congress should immediately repeal the Sherman Silver Purchase Act. He also said, in a letter to Assistant Secretary of the Treasury Charles S. Hamlin: "Of course the administration must be ready with some excellent substitute for the Sherman Law."

Cleveland hesitated at the water's edge. Instead of plunging in, he quietly instructed his cohorts that patronage promises were to be withheld from members of Congress who failed to promise to vote for repeal of the Sherman Silver Purchase Act. This placed civil service and tariff reform in the background.

Inauguration Day, March 4, came and went without a hint from Cleveland on when he might assume the initiative on the currency or any other problem. His brief inaugural address was conciliatory in tone and studded with platitudes and homely similes. "It behooves us," he said, to watch for every "symptom of insidious infirmity that threatens our national vigor." There was a brief reminder that any "exposure to degradation" of "a sound and stable currency" should "at once arouse to activity the most enlightened statesmanship." He dwelt more lengthily on the "unwholesome progeny of paternalism."

As in his famous Texas Seed bill veto message of 1886, he stated that "while the people should patriotically and cheerfully support their Government its functions do not include the support of the people." But he did make one exception to this rule, urging fair treatment of Indians — "the nation's wards." Cleveland mentioned monopolies, pledging that "to the extent that they can be reached and restrained by Federal power the General Government should relieve our citizens from their interference and exactions." But he did not define the proper "extent" of the federal government's reach, nor mention the Sherman Antitrust Act. His discussion of the tariff was vague and centered on reform in order to achieve "a more just and equitable system of Federal taxation." In contrast to his inaugural address of eight years before, which emphasized above all else the need for honest and efficient administration, this message contained no mention of civil service reform or any of the "good government" aims.

Ten days later news broke that the Philadelphia & Reading Railroad had gone bankrupt. Within another six weeks, on April 22, the Treasury surplus for the first time dropped below $100,000,000. Soon, on May 4, the National Cordage Company collapsed. Prices on the stock market, meanwhile, sank precipitously. As hoarding advanced, currency rapidly disappeared from circulation. In every large city there was a run on safety deposit vaults. Gold flowed rapidly to Europe. Credit dried up. During May and June many Western and Southern banks failed because Eastern banks were unable to provide them with cash in exchange for mortgages and other certificates of indebtedness.

Jim Hill wrote to Cleveland, June 15, from the St. Paul headquarters of his Great Northern Railway, reporting on the dire plight of country banks, including many "which have been considered entirely strong" and which "themselves thought they would be abundantly able to pull through." Hill also reported that he had made "careful enquiry along over five hundred miles of our lines as to the ability of the farmers to find the necessary money to pay for their binding twine, and the little they need for harvest help." The result of his inquiry was that "but very few of the farmers have any money, and the local banks are unable to aid them."

As to the remedy, Hill implied that he agreed with the movement for unconditioned repeal of the Sherman Silver Purchase Act. The business organizations throughout the West, Hill said, "feel the great difficulty now is want of confidence." Three weeks later, however, Hill doubted that repeal would be enough. He suggested to Cleveland that "if it is true that the circulating medium of the country, per capita, is too low . . . would it not be well received by the country" if bonds were issued "to meet a portion of the large [Civil War] pension appropriation"? These, Hill added, "would furnish a basis for National Bank [Note] Circulation." He also mentioned the lack of flexibility in the existing currency system and closed with the observation that he could "see no objection to an income tax," but at the same time thought it would be so difficult to enforce that it would become "very unpopular within a short time after it is put in effect."

The public and its leaders were understandably confused as to the causes of the panic and how to combat it.

People seemed unable to clear their minds of the jumble of conflicting notions and ideas that bred upon their fears, political affiliations, economic assumptions, and their property-holding and job-holding status. But gradually a crystallization took place, as men grasped at the most conspicuous panaceas at hand. More people than ever were attracted to the free-silver currency crusade: and more people than ever gravitated toward the gold currency fortress. In these movements, some politicians led and some followed, but few were any longer free to sit on the fence.

Cleveland was the most important individual driven from panic to panaceas. Supported by most politicians close to him, he decided to focus the Democratic party's activity on the currency question rather than on the tariff, "good government" or antimonopoly reforms. It was Cleveland, again supported by most politicians close to him, who chose the time and nature of this concentration. He waited until the gravity of the situation and public interest in the issue reached a high point. Then, on June 30, he called for a special session of Congress to meet August 7 to repeal the Sherman Silver Purchase Act. He believed the unpopularity of that measure, combined with a tough-minded use of the patronage whip, would result in uncompromising repeal. He decided not to recommend or support any one of the various suggested alternatives designed to provide an increase in the currency supply and at the same time satisfy politicians. He naturally ignored the Populists' Subtreasury plan, but he also ignored international bimetallism and the suggestion that the currency be backed by government bonds issued for that purpose or by other securities. Cleveland ignored the recommendation in the Democratic platform for repeal of the ten per cent federal tax on paper currency issued by state banks, and he did not consider a more limited silver purchase plan than that prescribed by the existing law.

Cleveland's insistence on unconditional repeal reflected his great faith that such good results would ensue that no substitute currency legislation would be necessary, at least for the time being. The immediate need was for confidence, and that confidence could be restored by determination to protect property values from ruin. He reasoned that if the government could dispel people's fear that they might get caught holding worthless, or near-worthless, currency, they would cease their scramble to get gold in exchange for intrinsically less valuable silver certificates, silver-backed treasury notes, greenbacks and bank notes. Lack of confidence in the currency he thought was due to the monthly increase in the supply of Treasury notes, issued because of the Sherman Silver Purchase Act. The public presumably feared that the Treasury could not long continue to exchange such a large, and ever-increasing, amount of notes for gold. Hence, Cleveland's remedy lay in repeal of the Sherman Silver Purchase Act.

But suddenly, before his decision to call Congress into special session was made public, a crisis threatened Cleveland's plan. The President had to undergo a serious operation for cancer, which might not be successful. Cleveland and the very few persons who were aware of the impending operation feared that if news of it leaked out the Treasury would be unable to meet the resulting requests for gold. In that event the nation would be off the gold standard. Public fear that Vice-President Adlai

Stevenson would be in command would cause a mad scramble for gold. Cleveland's prestige and his patronage whip might succeed in Congress, but silverite Stevenson would not even try to save the gold standard.

In early May Cleveland had noticed a rough spot on the roof of his mouth. By mid-June he was distressed enough to seek medical attention. An examination on June 18 revealed that Cleveland had a malignant growth the size of a quarter of a dollar from the molar teeth to almost the middle of the mouth. It encroached slightly on the soft palate, and there was some diseased bone. An immediate operation was vitally necessary. To insure secrecy, the few people aware of the situation arranged that the operation be performed aboard the yacht *Oneida,* which belonged to his Buzzards Bay friend and neighbor Commodore E. C. Benedict. On the evening of June 30, the same day that his call for a special session of Congress was announced, Cleveland and the Lamonts boarded the yacht at a New York pier. Next morning the yacht steamed slowly up the East River and the operation was begun on the fifty-six-year-old President. The doctors feared the effect on him of the anesthetic. In their opinion he was just the right build for a stroke of apoplexy — far too heavy, with a short, thick neck. But the operation was successful. Five days later the *Oneida* arrived at Buzzards Bay, and Cleveland walked with little apparent effort to his summer residence. Later, after another minor operation, he was provided with an artificial jaw of vulcanized rubber. Neither his facial appearance nor the quality of his voice was thereby altered. But he seemed less rugged and more irritable, and he weighed less.

The elaborate precautions for secrecy were so successful that it was a quarter of a century before the public learned the full story of the operation. Of the Cabinet members, only Lamont knew of it. True, a few weeks after the operation the story was reported in a Philadelphia newspaper, but it was emphatically denied by persons close to Cleveland. One of the doctors who assisted at the operation later said that he did more lying then than in all the rest of his active life put together. A close friend of Cleveland's, L. Clarke David, wrote to the Philadelphia *Public Ledger,* August 31, 1893: "I have seen the President at intervals since he first came to Buzzards Bay this summer, passing hours and days in his company and in the boat fishing with him. I passed all of last Monday with him, fishing, and I have never seen him in better health — never stronger, physically or mentally, and I consider him in both respects the healthiest man I know."

While Cleveland was still recuperating at Buzzards Bay, Congress began debate on the question of repeal of the Sherman Silver Purchase Act, and leaders on both sides marshaled their ablest talent to battle. In the House conspicuous roles for the repeal forces were played by majority leader William L. Wilson, Bourke Cockran and Thomas B. Reed. For the silverite cause Richard Bland and William Jennings Bryan were at the forefront. In the course of the debate, Bryan delivered his first great speech. The House show was dramatic, but not crucial, for the outcome was never in serious doubt. On the final vote, August 28, the repeal forces triumphed by 239 to 108.

In the Senate it appeared for a while that a spirit of compromise might prevail. Most of the Democrats, being practical professional politicians, feared that unconditional repeal would raise havoc with the already precarious party unity. Many of them also felt the need for a face-saving measure, for they had voted for the Sherman Silver Purchase Act in 1890 and now would have difficulty in explaining a complete reversal to their constituents. They discussed a reduction in the amount of silver to be purchased each month and continuance of purchases to some such future specified date as October, 1894. Gorman led the compromise movement among the Democrats, and John Sherman encouraged Republicans in that direction. By mid-October, after the debate had dragged on interminably, it was apparent that Senate sentiment overwhelmingly favored compromise.

It was Cleveland's turn to act. But his action was unfortunate. Though his message calling a special session of Congress bluntly made it clear that he was for unconditional repeal, many Senators hoped he would recognize political reality and cooperate. Vilas alone thought otherwise.

During most of October the impression prevailed in the Senate that Cleveland certainly would accept a compromise measure. "If he does not," said Sherman, "he will destroy his party, and his administration will be broken down." On October 16, the Steering Committee considered sending a delegation to Cleveland to discuss the question but dropped the matter when friends of the President warned that the visit might prove unsatisfactory for them. Finally Secretary Carlisle agreed to consult Cleveland and came back with the report that a compromise measure would not be acceptable.

Cleveland's reply did not end the compromise movement. Even though many Senators had pledged to support

Cleveland and had received patronage in return, they hoped that he would relent enough to make possible the passage of something less severe than unconditional repeal. Voorhees was one of these Senators, who as late as 1892 was a silverite but now was a Cleveland captive. On October 21, to emphasize their wishes, all but six or seven of the forty-four Democrats in the Senate endorsed a compromise plan presented by Gorman. It included such provisions as the extension of silver purchases until October 1, 1894. The notion still persisted that Cleveland would cooperate.

There were nevertheless some reasons to doubt that Cleveland would yield to the pressure. Politically he believed unconditional surrender was the strongest position. Back in August he had expressed the view to Vilas that if the Democrats failed to support unconditional repeal the Republicans would assume the lead. "I cannot help but feel," Cleveland said, "that there is a great danger of our friends the enemy gaining more credit with the country than we." By October he was certainly more than ever convinced that repeal would bring the greatest "credit with the country." Among the people he most respected, the business leaders, sentiment for unconditional repeal had stiffened. Some of them favored immediate legislation to provide for currency expansion and flexibility, but apparently the crisis had frightened them away from such schemes. In August, Higginson urged immediate repeal without a substitute. He expressed that view in one of his numerous letters to Hamlin, and then stated: "I believe in bi-metallism, and think it will follow when we put ourselves on the same basis as Europe. I have just been in New York two or three days, and find there a great many bi-metallists, representing America and Europe, and they all see clearly that we shall come to it through the repeal of the clause authorizing purchase of silver. Delay is immensely dangerous."

On October 23, at the time the Senate compromise effort reached a climax, William P. Thompson reported to Senator Johnson N. Camden, his brother-in-law, on the probability of compromise as viewed in New York business circles. Thompson was president of the National Lead Trust and a director of the Standard Oil Company. "The people over here," he stated, "are well informed, and nothing is ever started over in Washington that is not known of in a few minutes here." Thompson, who was no admirer of Cleveland, added that Cleveland could not be relied upon to carry out any promise he might have made to the compromisers. "He is seeking a certain kind of popularity, and will back out of a proposition just as quickly as he finds it is going to bring him into disfavor with a certain class or classes."

On that same day, October 23, Cleveland gave an emphatic answer to the wavering Senators. At a Cabinet meeting he smote the table with his fist and refused to yield an inch. A statement to that effect was issued to the public. The compromise movement collapsed, and a week later the long debate ended. On October 30 the vote on the repeal measure was taken. The result was 48 for and 37 against. The Democrats split 22 to 22. Cleveland, supported by more Republicans than Democrats, had succeeded.

Cleveland had won a great victory that led to a great defeat. Repeal of the Sherman Silver Purchase Act failed to end the financial crisis, which in turn contributed immeasurably to the ultimate demise of Bourbon supremacy in the Democratic party. The stark, irrefutable fact soon became apparent that repeal did not restore confidence. The Treasury surplus was $95,485,413. Just one year later it was down to $64,873,025 and continued to slide. At the same time there was a corresponding increase in the clamor for free silver.

Even though the depression became more and more severe during 1894 and 1895 and even though some of the less doctrinaire members of the Bourbon Democracy recognized the need for an active crusade for currency reform, Cleveland failed to supply effective leadership. Had he sought to create a middle ground for his party, he most certainly would have had the cooperation of most of his party leaders. Sometime during 1893 and 1894, for example, Whitney became converted, and with enthusiasm, to international bimetallism. But he found it impossible to arouse Cleveland to a like interest in the movement. There was no other place for Democrat Whitney to go for effective political sponsorship of his views, so he remained a loyal defender of Cleveland.

Cleveland was well aware of the need for more currency and for a better banking system. He was also aware of several plans designed to reform without driving gold out of the country or into private hoarding. But he adopted a defeatist attitude toward them. On the eve of the 1894 election, doubtless in answer to a Whitney attempt to interest the President in international bimetallism, Cleveland wrote gloomily that he had been watching the "drift of sentiment touching a wider use of silver in the countries but I am afraid it has not advanced far enough in our country to be useful, though an international agree-

ment has been my hope for some time past." Without
suggesting the possibility that he himself had an obligation to exert leadership in an effort to achieve international agreement, Cleveland went on to say that the nation would never be in a "good state of national health
until we retrace our steps and separate more the operation of the Government from the business of the people."
He felt that if "we could have a safe system of State banking which would or might under proper restrictions put
out good safe money that would gradually replace and
cause the retirement of Government issues which threaten
our gold, it might be a step in the right direction." But
he was very discouraged and at a loss to know what to say
on the financial situation in his annual message. "I am
not sure," he remarked, "that I shall be able to prepare
any comprehensive financial plan and it may appear best
to attempt to bridge over until the new Congress convenes
in long session." In his annual message, Cleveland did
recommend banking reform that would allow some restricted issue of notes by state banks. But his plan was too
mild and his personal manner too spiritless to place him
in a position of effective leadership.

To insure a gold reserve in the Treasury sufficient to
continue the gold standard, Cleveland used the borrow-
ing power of the government. He had the Treasury sell
bonds to private sources for gold. Many people doubted
the legality of this practice, but when the anti-Cleveland
majority in Congress refused his request for legislative
authority, he used earlier vague laws as a justification.
Twice during 1894, once in 1895 and once in 1896 Secretary Carlisle issued gold bonds.

The nature of the 1895 gold bond sales emphasized the

unsatisfactory state of the Cleveland-Bourbon financial program, and that fact was not overlooked by reform-minded enemies of Cleveland. The bonds were handled, at a substantial profit, by a syndicate of bankers, headed by J. P. Morgan. The experience of earlier gold bond sales had taught that if the process of continued bond issuance was to end in the foreseeable future more was needed than a simple exchange for gold. Some action had to be taken to restrain bankers from making large demands on the gold reserve by presenting paper money to the Treasury, and the nation's supply of gold needed to be increased. Hence, in making arrangements for the 1895 gold purchase of some $62,000,000, Morgan promised Cleveland that at least half of the gold would be purchased abroad and that the members of the syndicate would make every effort to avoid draining the gold out of the Treasury. Many citizens were shocked by this evidence that the government at Washington was so dependent upon the power of one man in Wall Street. Nor did it help matters when they contemplated the implications of the large profit of Morgan and his associates. The gold purchases proved sufficient to tide the Treasury over until the devastating depression finally ran its course, and late in 1896 the economy began an upward climb that was not seriously interrupted until 1907. Only after the panic of that year did the nation seek and find a greatly improved approach to the ancient currency-banking problem.

While Cleveland doggedly, stubbornly struggled to maintain gold payments, he also faced other serious problems. He wrestled with the tariff, with imperialism in Hawaii, with a crisis involving the striking workingmen of the Pullman Company, and with the Venezuela-British Guiana boundary dispute. There was drama here — realistic exposure of faults in the social fabric of the era and an indication of the future course of American civilization. In a sense these events overshadowed in importance the principal actor — Grover Cleveland. They were somehow anticlimactic in his political career. With the accomplishment of unconditional repeal of the Sherman Silver Purchase Act, Cleveland had used his trump political card, and he simply had not enough strength left to overcome the sad results of that victory or to combat the other challenges that followed. Politically he had overplayed his hand, but to the bitter end he seemed unaware that he would not win on the final count. Cleveland and some of his fellow Bourbons kept telling each other that very soon the public would recognize the fallacy of following political heretics. He did not realize that he was fighting vainly to sustain a past against a future that would not be denied.

Hardly had Cleveland and Congress disposed of the Sherman Silver Purchase Act when they confronted the tariff question. Congress had the matter before it from the opening of the regular session in December, 1893, until August of the following year. The House tariff reformers were much more successful than those of the Senate. Majority leader Wilson steered a moderate reform measure through to passage in the House. The Wilson Bill aimed to reduce the average duties from the fortynine per cent of the high McKinley Act to about thirty per cent. The measure made many concessions to protectionism, but it also included a long free list of raw and unfinished materials. Also to compensate for the expected loss of revenue under the new schedules, the Wilson Bill and the measure which was finally enacted into law included provision for a tax on personal income.

The main battle was in the Senate, where a large and powerful combination of Republican and Democratic protectionists conducted a determined drive to check reform. By the time the measure became the Wilson-Gorman Act, it was a far cry from genuine reform. Cleveland was bitterly disappointed and let the bill become law without his signature.

Cleveland contributed to this failure. He had exhausted his patronage strength in getting Senators to repeal the Sherman Silver Purchase Act. His personal political ineptness antagonized many Senators who otherwise might have cooperated with their party chief. Never popular with most politicians, Cleveland had irritated the Senators by his refusal to compromise. Then, just before the question was considered in the Senate, he violated the senatorial courtesy tradition by nominating a New Yorker, William B. Hornblower, for the Supreme Court without consulting the New York Senators. The nominee, moreover, was a political enemy of Senator Hill. When the Senate Judiciary Committee refused to confirm the appointment, Cleveland nominated another New Yorker, Wheeler H. Peckham, equally unacceptable to Hill. Finally, after defeat on this name, he bowed to senatorial courtesy, and Senator Edward D. White received the post. Senator Vilas, a loyal Cleveland supporter on the Judiciary Committee, apologized to the committee for Cleveland's performance. Vilas reminded the committee that Cleveland had the habit of great independence. Congressman Wilson, who felt bitterly disappointed in the tariff outcome, in 1897 confided to his diary how he felt about Cleveland's relationship with House and Senate members. Wilson regarded Cleveland as woefully "lacking in the tact of making ordinary men and especially representative public men feel a personal friendship and personal loyalty to him by little social and conventional attentions. Always courteous, frequently kindly, always frank and business-like he yet did not seem to think of the power he had, and possibly the duty he was under, to tie men to him by personal ties, rather than by political or business relations." Wilson felt that Cleveland could have kept many members of Congress personally friendly "by a casual invitation to lunch, or a formal invitation to dinner, a stroll together or a carriage drive."

In his relations with the Senate on the specific matter of the Wilson-Gorman Tariff bill Cleveland exhibited his usual ineptitude. He managed to arouse to a high pitch the anger of the Gorman-led Democratic protectionists in the Senate. This group held the balance of power, so the tariff reformers needed their cooperation if a satisfactory reform measure was to be enacted. The bill that was passed in the Senate, then sent to the House and finally to a Senate-House conference committee was a far cry from the original Wilson bill. The Senate had greatly shortened the free list and markedly increased the duties on scores of protected items. While this protectionist measure was being discussed in the House, Cleveland made a blunt attack on the Gorman group. In a letter written for public consumption Cleveland called upon the House to reject the Senate measure because this bill violated the principles and promises of the Democratic party and therefore was a product of "party perfidy and party dishonor."

Cleveland thought he was delivering a master political stroke, but the actual result was to end whatever chance he had of obtaining a decent compromise. His outburst afforded Gorman a pretext indignantly to defy Cleveland. The President doubtless would have done better to strike out boldly against the pressure being exerted by the lobbyists representing powerful business groups, instead of condemning a powerful segment of his own party. Very much in evidence were representatives of the National Lead Trust, Standard Oil, coal interests, the Havemeyer's Sugar Trust and many others. At least a few Senators, moreover, speculated in sugar at the same time they were raising the sugar duty. Senator Matthew Quay of Pennsylvania admitted doing so, but he added that it was nobody's business but his own and that he would continue the practice if it pleased his fancy.

Although the tariff act that finally emerged lowered rates from those prevailing under the McKinley Act, it nevertheless represented a distinct victory for the high protectionists. It was a sad ending to the crusade Cleveland had launched in 1887. Cleveland's defeat marked the end of the reform phase of his public career. Problems arising out of the economic situation had blunted the edge of his "good government" crusade. And now, a combination of powerful opponents and Cleveland's own inept and faltering performance brought his tariff reform efforts to the end of the road. Henceforth, as President and Democratic party chieftain, he narrowed his role to that of a bold protector of the *status quo*.

I X
Defender of the *Status Quo*

CLEVELAND was much more successful as a defender of the *status quo* than as a crusader for change. The constitutional power to veto legislation, to issue orders to subordinate appointive officials and even to send the military forces into action were at his command as chief executive. The judiciary was staffed with enough conservatives to help sustain the Bourbon concepts. Cleveland could exercise his considerable power without consulting the public or the representatives of the public — in and out of office. He could perform as his imperious self; and he did.

Three times during 1894, while the tariff question was still in the legislative mill, Cleveland used his great power to frustrate organized challenges to Bourbonism. In March he vetoed the Seigniorage bill, which represented a compromise between the gold and silver forces. His refusal to accept this measure served notice that he was unimpressed by the arguments favoring an increase in the supply of currency and that he would not bow to political expediency. This veto added fuel to the fire of discontent in the agrarian areas, where the free-silver blaze spread faster than ever before.

The other two episodes that brought forth the iron fist were an outgrowth of the widespread suffering, frustration and anger prevalent among the wage earners of the nation. These feelings found expression in many ways, but they reached the attention of Cleveland with most emphasis through the "petition in boots" of unemployed persons banded together in Coxey's Army and through organized labor's boycott of the railroads that resulted from a strike of the Pullman Company workers.

Previous to these events Cleveland as President had avoided close contact with wage-earner protests. In the days of his governorship of New York he had been confronted with wage-earner pressure for remedial legislation, but his accession to the Presidency had placed him out of direct reach of such pressure. Champions of labor, unlike champions of farmers, had not yet acquired enough power to make effective demands on the dominant national political leadership. During his first term in the Presidency, Cleveland remained at a safe distance from the excitement engendered by the eight-hour movment of 1886. His one contribution was a halfhearted suggestion to Congress that it establish a compulsory arbitration tribunal. In 1892, when the presidential campaign was on and when, at the same time, a strike at Homestead resulted in shocking strife, Cleveland remained stonily silent. But now, in the sad depression year of 1894, he found himself confronted not only by angry agrarian silverites but also by angry organized wage earners.

Of the various demonstrations of protest by desperate unemployed citizens, the one that came almost literally

to Cleveland's doorstep was Coxey's Army, or the "petition in boots." Since 1892 Jacob S. Coxey, of Massillon,
Ohio, had earnestly sought support for his Good Roads
bill — a public works measure to provide jobs for the unemployed. His project was to be financed through government bonds, which would serve as collateral for $500,000,-
000 in newly issued paper currency. In the spring of 1894
Coxey and a few hundred unemployed citizens drama-
tized their plight by marching en masse to the national
capital. Upon their arrival mounted police, in accordance
with the plans of law enforcer Olney, rudely dispersed
the petitioners and put Coxey in jail for a brief time.
During and after the march of this "living petition," the
spokesmen of some citizens who did have jobs and property employed both ridicule and scare tactics to discredit
the movement. While there was nothing "anarchistic"
or even militant about these ragged and footsore petitioners, there was enough ridiculous showmanship sprinkled
into Coxey's Army to afford dogma-bound editorial writ-
ers material to brand the crusade as a huge joke.

Though Olney and Cleveland showed no interest in
unemployment other than to use force to protect persons
and property from destruction at the hands of desperate
victims of the depression, Congress made a gesture toward doing more. When the Coxey movement was at its
height, Congress created a Select Committee on Public
Distress. A Milwaukee *Journal* correspondent, after talk-
ing with the committee chairman, Vilas, reported that
"there was a general feeling about the senate that it
would become necessary to formulate some measure that
would in some way meet the conditions which seemed
to exist." But as it turned out, with the advent of the

Pullman boycott, said Vilas, "conditions changed so quickly . . . that it soon became evident that the committee would not be called upon to do much." Public interest soon veered to the Pullman drama. The concern of Congress was seemingly not fear of the unemployed themselves but of pressure from mounting public sympathy for the unemployed.

In 1894, when a strike in Pullman, Illinois, led to a large-scale power struggle between organized employers and organized laborers, Cleveland unhesitatingly threw the tremendous power at his disposal to the side of the employers. The Pullman strike began in May, 1894, when 4,000 workers in a plant manufacturing railway cars went on strike. In June the American Railway Union, headed by Eugene V. Debs, promised to aid the Pullman workers by inaugurating a boycott; and the General Managers' Association, made up of officials from twenty-four railroads, allied with the Pullman company. The boycott, carried on by railway workers who refused to handle Pullman cars, started in Chicago and spread rapidly. In July the federal government entered conspicuously upon the scene, armed with two powerful weapons — the injunction and armed force. The injunction was a federal court order, which in this case directed Debs and his associates to cease their support of the boycott; the federal troops were to insure public order.

Cleveland made the decisions and thereby assumed the responsibility for federal action taken to end the boycott; but it was Attorney General Olney who initiated and carried out the plan. The Cleveland-Olney relationship in handling the Pullman boycott, and in other matters also, was a remarkable example of efficient and effective administrative teamwork. It combined a clear division of labor with mutual understanding and respect. While Cleveland was engrossed in the Wilson-Gorman Tariff struggle, Olney concentrated on the Pullman boycott. Olney was well prepared by inclination and by knowledge to launch an aggressive drive against the demands of the rising tide of organized railway workers. Having been an important railroad attorney, he was well aware that trouble with railroad workers had been brewing for several years, and at the same time he saw but one solution. To him labor unions were a dangerous blight on free enterprise. Whatever personal sympathy he might have had for the plight of workingmen and their families and whatever private thoughts he might have had about the highhandedness of George Pullman in dealing with the obviously just complaints of the workers, Olney's philosophy did not permit him to allow such considerations to govern his actions.

Olney's determination to win the battle against organized labor was so intense that he cast aside whatever scruples he had as to the legal justification for his action. He concluded that the most effective legal advice for stopping the boycott was to obtain an injunction from a judge restraining the activity of Debs and his cohorts. This would make it possible to jail and fine the offenders if they defied the injunction. Olney found authority for this device in the Sherman Antitrust Act. Many people were surprised and angered at this interpretation of the Act, but they were in no position to do more than to protest or to defy the government with physical force.

Olney forestalled serious violence by seeing to it that federal troops were sent into the Chicago area, and

wherever else trouble might arise. The dispatch of troops
likewise surprised and angered many people, but again
they were without effective means to combat the action.
The most conspicuous protester was popular John P.
Altgeld, Democratic Governor of Illinois. He wrote vehemently to Cleveland, who had issued the troop order at
the behest of Olney. The incensed Altgeld reminded
Cleveland that under the law the President had no right
to order soldiers to the scene, and he presented detailed
information to show that local and state authorities were
in complete mastery of the situation. He assured Cleveland that there was no threat to public safety, to the
normal transportation of the mail or to the conduct of the
federal courts. Cleveland was unimpressed by the arguments of his fellow Democrat. Clearly Olney had not
furnished his chief with a balanced picture of the conditions in Illinois, perhaps assuming that such details were
merely incidental to the all-important need to end the
irresponsible and dangerous effrontery of Debs and his
band of labor conspirators.

The disciplinary action against organized labor was
successful but politically costly. Not only did Cleveland
and Olney end the Debs-led boycott, but upon being
sustained by the conservative Supreme Court in their use
of an injunction, they were powerfully armed to suppress
future union defiance of the prevailing economic pattern.
Their action, however, aroused many laborers and friends
of labor to spirited opposition.

For Cleveland and the Bourbons, the enmity of Altgeld
brought especially grave political consequences. Altgeld
emerged from the Pullman boycott obssessed with a determination to drive Cleveland and Bourbonism from

control of the national Democratic party. Previous to the
strike Altgeld had refrained from active participation in
national politics, though his ambition had been to enter
the United States Senate. With this purpose in mind he
had concentrated his efforts on political fence building in the Illinois Democracy. He was an adroit, highly
intelligent, personable, enlightened, reform-minded politician. Although he was not above using the tricks of the
professional politician, he was not a mere timeserver and
opportunist. In short, he was a politician-statesman.
During his campaigns for the governorship in 1892 and
subsequently, Altgeld had carefully developed a large and
loyal following among Illinois voters and politicians. He
knew how to use his German background to please Ger-
man-American voters, and he knew how to speak the
language and champion the causes of farmers, businessmen and laborers. His pardon of the Haymarket anar-
chists brought him a reputation for courage and gained
him more support among laborers than it lost among
shocked conservatives. And now, in 1894, with his reputation among laborers greatly enhanced by his role in the
Pullman strike, he sallied forth upon the national political battleground. The likelihood that Altgeld might lead
the vote-strong Illinois Democracy out of the Bourbon
camp was especially ominous for the political fortunes of
the Bourbon Democrats.

But many people approved of the Cleveland-Olney approach to the labor crisis. James J. Hill, the "empire
builder," had especial reason for elation over the outcome because, just previous to the Pullman boycott,
Debs's union had won a strike against wage cuts on the
Great Northern Railroad. Hill reported to Lamont

that "the public, without reference to party lines, are unanimous in approving and supporting the action of the President" in his defiance of Altgeld. "As I heard one of the judges in our Supreme Court say: 'There is a higher law, even if it comes to the law of necessity.' Whatever else the public may think, they will always approve prompt and courageous action in behalf of the country."

As he stolidly fought back each succeeding wave of anti-Bourbonism, Cleveland became increasingly morose. The mid-term election results, marked by notable Republican and moderate Populist gains, did not upset him as much as subsequent developments. There was nothing disturbing about a political setback for a party in power during a depression, but the continuance of the economic crisis itself through 1895 and 1896 was not conducive to happiness.

Cleveland was especially concerned over the mounting popularity of the free-silver movement, but he nevertheless was slow to admit defeat. For a long time he believed that the Bourbon-dominated Democratic organizations in the South would keep that region in line. As for the West, the Bourbons were clearly in serious trouble. Some of his friends attempted to bolster Cleveland's spirits. "How 'do the heathen rage and the people imagine 'a vain thing' in the silver lunacy?" wrote Vilas in May, 1895, to Cleveland. "It is the effervescence of folly. The conditions daily improve, thanks in part to that excellent contract last made for gold, and, by the Autumn change of conditions will do for public judgment what reason never does in adversity, reduce it to wisdom in its resultant." Cleveland himself in the same month wrote to his wealthy friend Benedict that he could not believe that the Democratic party would become committed to free silver. But he was "afraid there will be such nibbling and fussing with it that we will be discredited and suspected, however much next year we protest the soundness and safety of our views."

Cleveland was also deeply hurt by the steady deterioration of his relationship with politicians in his own party. Added to the longstanding widespread dislike for Cleveland among professional politicians was their conviction that Cleveland's uncompromising attitude was ruining the party and their own political fortunes. Senator Brice, for example, remarked in May, 1896, that he did not "propose to pull any more chestnuts out of the fire for Grover Cleveland." Many Democratic members of the House and Senate were especially irritated. In a letter to Ambassador Bayard in February, 1895, the lonely President said: "Think of it! Not a man in the Senate with whom I can be on terms of absolute confidence. Our Wisconsin friend [Vilas] and former associate seems somehow to be cowed, and our Delaware friend [Gray] has only spasmodic self assertion and generally is in doubt as to the correctness of what I do or want to do." Vilas and Gray had certainly not forsaken Cleveland, but doubtless they had their moments of discouragement as they defended him against the jibes of fellow Senators.

Cleveland sought solace outside the world of public affairs whenever time permitted. He wrote movingly to Benedict, in answer to a kind word from his friend: "Such expressions are my only comfort, except my wife and babies, in these troublous perplexing days." And more frequently than previously he made references to the guidance of God and to his "supreme faith in the American people." Aside from the joys of family life and his occasional vacationing at Buzzards Bay, his only pleasure seemed to come from his personal financial dealings. Benedict, who managed these details for him and advised him on investments, received frequent letters from Cleveland on the subject. In one, dated in February, 1895, the President remarked that "half the fun of holding stocks and bonds is to see if their value increase or decrease. In one case a calm satisfaction intervenes — in the other the exhilaration of hope and expectation." Three months later, after informing Benedict that he still had "twelve or fifteen thousand dollars which ought to be earning something," Cleveland added that he was "developing quite a strong desire to make money," and that he thought it was "a good time to indulge in that propensity."

Although 1893 and 1894 were troublous years for the Bourbons, even sadder ones followed. During 1895 and into 1896 the Democrats suffered from an especially critical intraparty struggle between the Bourbons and the silverite element for control of the party. The Bourbon Democracy found it more difficult than at any time previously to cling to control. The pressure from below was so strong and persistent that eventually the Bourbon group suffered total political disability. Several factors contributed to this outcome: widespread public disillusionment with their leadership as the depression persisted; the obtuseness of Cleveland himself; and the increasing effectiveness of free silver as a rallying point for disaffected politicians, voters and silver mine operators.

Cleveland, by reason of his official position and his refusal to accept the counsel of wiser Democrats than him-

self, was to a large degree to blame for the collapse of
the Bourbon Democracy. He had ignored the opportunities to divert the attention of influential politicians and
many voters away from free silver. In 1895 it may already have been too late to save the Bourbons, but
certainly Cleveland could have performed more in accord
with the rules of politics — his chosen profession. As President he should have taken action to reform the decrepit
currency-banking system, and there were plenty of plans
he might have championed at a time when the silverites
had pushed their opponents into a compromise mood.

Whitney was the recipient of several compromise suggestions. His earlier conversion to international bimetallism and his influential political position made him the
potential savior of the party. In June, 1896, the Assistant
Secretary of the Treasury Hamlin sent Whitney some
suggestions he had received for the "possible conversion
of several free silver men." "I would also suggest for your
consideration," Hamlin added, "the advisability of offering to the Convention a plank providing for free banking
. . . under uniform National regulation." The banks
could issue notes, "not to be legal tender." Hamlin believed: "As against the cry of 'Free Silver,' we can offer
'free banking' with hope of influencing some delegates
without sacrificing principle."

International bimetallists also continued to press for
their plan. Some members of this group believed that
the United States might be able to overcome that formi-
dable obstacle to international agreement that emanated
from the powerful British group led by Lord Arthur
Balfour. One leading English international bimetallist
wrote Whitney a scorching criticism of Cleveland and,

after urging his pet reform, added that even free silver would improve the situation for the United States: it might cause a temporary crisis, but a great increase in American exports would soon follow. But nobody of importance seemed to have the temerity to suggest, at least for the record, that a campaign for international bimetallism might well attract a tremendously large number of voters. Not only was it a more moderate approach than free silver, but it afforded an opportunity for politicians to place the blame for the nation's plight on greedy Britain, the greatest foreign obstacle to international agreement.

It was of course to his credit that Cleveland did not stoop to a deliberate use of superpatriotism to attain public favor. But if he sincerely favored international agreement on silver, there was no reason why he should have shrunk from incurring British disfavor through a bold advocacy of the plan. Clearly Cleveland's negative, defeatist approach to international bimetallism reflected more than anything else his stubborn pride that prevented him from voluntary change or conspicuous concessions.

In 1895 one event, the Venezuela boundary dispute, showed the political advantage of international issues as a means of gaining popularity with the voters. Cleveland's actions in that controversy were clearly not motivated by partisan considerations, but his audacious conduct brought more public acclaim than he ever received on the domestic front. The episode was less important for its ultimate effect on the nation's foreign relations than for its revelation of the American public temper and the peculiar approach to diplomacy employed by Cleveland and Secretary of State Olney.

There had been a long-standing dispute between Venezuela and Great Britain over the boundary between Venezuela and British Guiana. The United States, in response to a request of Venezuela and presumably in accordance with the Monroe Doctrine, used its influence to persuade Great Britain to come to terms. Cleveland finally lost patience. On the advice of Olney, who had become Secretary of State after the death of Gresham, Cleveland dispatched a blistering note to Lord Balfour. The message could easily have been interpreted as a threat of war unless Britain yielded to American demands. The British were as displeased as superpatriotic Americans were elated, but Lord Balfour refrained from answering in kind. Finally the boundary dispute was settled by an arbitration commission, and with results almost in complete accord with the original British claims.

The episode was out of keeping with the usual course followed by Cleveland and his State Department. During both his administrations, Cleveland had pursued a restrained and dignified, but at the same time firm, course. He had been anything but aggressive. And while other nations became increasingly imperialistic, Cleveland definitely did not. When the growing imperialistic impulse in America brought the nation to the verge of the annexation of Hawaii, Cleveland had forthrightly reversed the movement. He withdrew from the Senate a pending treaty to confirm annexation. Doubtless Cleveland's bluntness in the Venezuela matter developed from the personal irritability that accompanied his discouraging experiences in national affairs and, more important, his unthinking acceptance of advice from Olney.

Cleveland had within easy reach opportunities to please

the public that were unrelated to the heated currency controversy and that were aimed at the public good. In 1895 the Supreme Court incurred the wrath of countless citizens by declaring the income tax provision of the Wilson-Gorman Tariff Act unconstitutional, in a strange five to four decision. This was the most controversial action of the Court since the 1857 Dred Scott decision. Even many moderates were shocked by the event. But while income tax advocates noisily condemned the decision, Cleveland remained silent. His belief that it was unseemly to criticize the Court constrained him from joining the attack, but he might at least have joined forces with those persons who urged repair of the damage through an income tax amendment to the Constitution. His silence gave plausibility to the charge that Cleveland, along with the Court, was a servant of the "Wall Street moneybags."

The monopoly problem afforded a large and beckoning opportunity for popular and needed reform. J. P. Morgan and others were exploiting business distress to form ever more monopolies, and correspondingly reformers were increasing their clamor. In 1894 one of Altgeld's Chicago friends, Henry Demarest Lloyd, had published *Wealth Against Commonwealth,* a devastating attack on the oil monopoly. This book received wide attention but apparently went unnoticed by Cleveland and his associates. Instead the Bourbons worried over the great popularity of another book published in 1894—a silverite tract called *Coin's Financial School,* by William P. Harvey.

The only notable action on the monopoly front was taken at the instigation of Olney while he was Attorney General. The result aided rather than retarded the growth of trusts, for it ended in a Supreme Court decision that so narrowed the government's authority under the Sherman Antitrust Act that several years were to transpire before that Act became a useful legal vehicle. The case in question, United States *vs*. E. C. Knight Company, involved the Sugar Trust. The Court sustained the trust and at the same time found occasion to provide a definition of federal power that left monopolies free to flourish unless they were very directly involved in interstate commerce. Antimonopolists charged, and the logic of events indicated, that they may well have been correct, that Olney deliberately presented a weak case to the Court. There was no denying that the government attorneys did present a weak case. It was likewise true that ex-railroad attorney Olney had no enthusiasm for the Sherman Antitrust Act—except as a basis for obtaining injunctions against labor union leaders. His enemies believed that Olney started the action against the Sugar Trust in the hope that the Sherman Antitrust Act would be declared unconstitutional.

Months before the event itself, it was apparent to most Democrats that only a near miracle could prevent the silverites from dislodging the Bourbons from party control when the contending forces converged in early July, 1896, at the national nominating convention. The Bourbons could not impress party members with their strength in the East, where in the 1894 election the key state of New York had moved emphatically into the Republican column. Professional politicians were much more impressed by events in the West and South. The attractiveness of free silver for mineowners and distraught farmers, Populist party gains, bitter anger at Cleveland and the Bourbons in general and the continuation of hard times caused

Bourbon prestige to dwindle uninterruptedly. The Bourbons were especially discouraged in the spring of 1895 when Altgeld induced the politically important Illinois Democracy to endorse free silver.

Frantic attempts to stem the tide simply made matters worse. The Bourbon tactic had been to induce Cleveland to write one of his letters—this time to the Honest Money League of Chicago. "Disguise it as we may," the President announced, "the line of battle is drawn between the forces of safe currency and those of silver monometallism." His statement caused many moderate Democrats, who hoped for a compromise, to get off the fence, and many more of them landed in the silver camp than on the gold side.

As the 1896 convention approached, the charming, popular Whitney took charge of the Bourbons. He disappointed many Democrats when he flatly refused to be a candidate for the nomination, but they were pleased when he consented to postpone a trip to Europe in order to lead them in the convention fight. In contrast to Cleveland, the politically wise Whitney sought to pull the Bourbons halfway back from the end of the currency limb. He rounded up key Bourbons, such as Vilas and Russell, to join forces with him at the national convention. He recognized that the silverites would have a majority of delegate strength, but he hoped to check them short of the two-thirds majority necessary for nomination of a candidate. That, he thought, would force the silverites to a compromise. Whitney hoped to obtain an endorsement of international bimetallism at the convention and the nomination of William E. Russell, able Bourbon Governor of Massachusetts.

But it was too late. Upon arrival in Chicago for the con-

vention, Whitney and the Bourbons in general were
stunned. They knew they would face a strong anti-Bourbon majority, but they had no idea it would be as strong
and as angry as that which actually greeted them. The
hostile mood was everywhere apparent at the convention,
and on hand to keep it alive and to give it positive direction were such able leaders as Altgeld, Bland and Bryan.
Altgeld appeared to be the most skillful manager, but
Bryan's was the voice that clarified for the delegates in
particular and the nation in general what the new leadership thought. Utilizing to the fullest his magnificent talent
for oratory, Bryan said of the Bourbons: "We have peti-
tioned, and our petitions have been scorned; we have en-
treated, and our entreaties have been disregarded; we have
begged, and they have mocked when our calamity came.
We beg no longer; we entreat no more; we petition no
more. We defy them."

The conclave turned into something of a family quar-
rel. The Bourbons, who for so long had dominated the
party, had run afoul of the depression of the 1890's, failing either to prevent hard times or to bring about the
return of good times. Bryan, defiant, and supported by
purposeful mineowners, was rewarded with the presidential nomination and the opportunity to lead the party
out of the wreckage of nineteenth-century Bourbonism.
But he and his compatriots had much to learn and much
to do before they could arrive at high-level constructive
statesmanship. In 1896 they possessed the proper spirit,
and in the free-silver proposal they had a popular issue.
But they needed a broader program, more in keeping
with the original Populist platform.

The Bourbon remnant believed that the new leaders
of the party could not survive the folly of their ways and

that Bourbonism would soon be back in the party saddle. After the 1896 nomination, a group of incensed Bourbons, including Cleveland, gave their support to Republican candidate William McKinley. That was uncomfortable, for McKinley was a high tariff Republican, and until Mark Hanna and political expediency had convinced him otherwise, he had been friendly to the free-silver cause. "Between us," wrote Olney to Cleveland following the nomination of McKinley and Bryan, "the difference is one of platforms and followers. So far as personal qualifications for the Presidency are concerned, I should as soon take my chance with Bryan as with McKinley."

The Bourbons, in order to avoid conspicuous contact with McKinley and his party but at the same time to lend him aid, established a national Democratic party. This group, with the blessing of Cleveland, held a convention and nominated a ticket. Hence, gold Democrats, who wanted to vote on election day but could not bring themselves to support a Republican, were able to help the cause by voting "Democratic" without voting for Bryan. They could vote for the Democratic ticket headed by presidential candidate John M. Palmer, elderly Senator from Illinois.

Although Cleveland and the others in the Bourbon remnant were pleased when McKinley defeated Bryan in November, they could not be really elated until the return of Bourbons and Bourbonism to command of the Democratic party. That time never came. Cleveland retired from active politics, to live quietly in Princeton, New Jersey, until he died in 1908. The other Bourbon leaders likewise slipped into political oblivion. As one of them wrote in 1900: "The Democratic party, as we knew it, is dead."

A Note on the Sources

THE BASIC manuscript collection used for this study was the Cleveland Papers (Library of Congress). The author also used the Papers of William E. Curtis, Charles E. Hamlin (including his Diary), Daniel S. Lamont and William C. Whitney (all in the Library of Congress). Material was used from the Ignatius Donnelly Papers (Minnesota Historical Society) and the William Freeman Vilas Papers (State Historical Society of Wisconsin).

In addition to the usual published collections of addresses, state papers and writings that accompany and follow the career of a President, there is a special published assemblage of material — Allan Nevins, *Letters of Grover Cleveland, 1850-1908* (1933). The present author discovered no letters of significance written by Cleveland, except for some very meaningful ones in the Whitney Papers, that are not included in this useful Nevins volume. The principal newspapers used for this study were the New York *Tribune,* the New York *Herald,* the New York *Times* and the New York *World.*

The most important biography of Cleveland is Allan Nevins, *Grover Cleveland, A Study in Courage* (1932). This detailed study is impressive for its arresting literary style and its broad scope. It is a storehouse of documented material. The present writer is indebted to Professor Nevins for the material he assembled and presented so vividly in this Pulitzer Prize biography. On several aspects of Cleveland's personality, views and actions, however, there are marked differences in interpretation between this volume and the Nevins biography. The only other life of Cleveland useful to serious students is the authorized work: Robert McElroy, *Grover Cleveland, The Man and the Statesman* (2 vols., 1923).

There are many books about important leaders and developments of the Cleveland era. The following abbreviated list is compiled on the basis of those which were especially useful in the preparation of this volume:

De Alva S. Alexander, *Four Famous New Yorkers, The Political Careers of Cleveland, Platt, Hill and Roosevelt* (1923); Harry Barnard, *"Eagle Forgotten," The Life of John Peter Altgeld* (1938); James A. Barnes, *John G. Carlisle, Financial Statesman* (1931); Mary R. Dearing, *Veterans in Politics, The Story of the G.A.R.* (1952); Chester McA. Destler, *American Radicalism, 1865-1901* (1946); Sidney Fine, *Laissez Faire and the General-Welfare State, A Study of Conflict in American Thought, 1865-1901* (1956); John D. Hicks, *The Populist Revolt* (1931); Richard Hofstadter, *The American Political Tradition* (1948), and also *The Age of Reform* (1955); Howard L. Hurwitz, *Theodore Roosevelt and Labor in New York State, 1880-1900* (1943); Mark C. Hirsch, *William C. Whitney: Modern Warwick* (1948); Matthew Josephson, *The Politicos, 1865-1896* (1938); John R. Lambert, *Arthur Pue Gorman* (1953); Almont Lindsey, *The Pullman Strike* (1942); Horace Samuel Merrill, *Bourbon Democracy of the Middle West, 1865-1896* (1953), and also *William Freeman Vilas, Doctrinaire Democrat* (1954); James C. Olson, *J. Sterling Morton* (1942); George F. Parker, *Recollections of Grover Cleveland* (1909); Harry Thurston Peck, *Twenty Years of the Republic* (1906); Fred A. Shannon, *The Farmers' Last Frontier, Agriculture, 1860-1897* (1945); Festus P. Summers, *William L. Wilson and Tariff Reform* (1953); Hans B. Thorelli, *The Federal Antitrust Policy, Origination of an American Tradition* (1955); Joseph Frazier Wall, *Henry Watterson, Reconstructed Rebel* (1956); and C. Vann Woodward, *Origins of the New South, 1877-1913* (1951).

Index